7-22-19

Ted —

Thought you might enjoy this quick read of the letters sent by a man to his fiancée during his service in the military. Years later, he found she had saved them all! The man is the cousin of my best friend.

Aloha — Joe

WEAPONS OF WAR

A compilation of letters recounting a
soldier's story of service, love, and faith.

Robert E. Wright
Indianapolis, Indiana 2018 by Robert E. Wright
ISBN: 9781977088673

To Angela and Nolise, so they will have a detailed and accurate account of how it all began.

To the Men and Women of the United States Armed Forces who are separated from their loved ones and families.

Deacon Wright,

Thank you for the privilege of reading "Weapons of War". I could not put it down, reading 75 pages a day over three days.

Anyone who knows me, knows that l only read and watch true stories: biography channel, history channel, investigative discovery channel and documentaries. Therefore, I speak with experience when I say "Weapons of War", is a captivating story of love, faith, duty and devotion.

Although I personally knew how the story would end, personal knowledge did not matter, I still found myself emotionally drawn into the story.

Your letters are so well-written until they pull the reader back into time and allowed him/her to share the moment with you. Your tribute letter to your wife and her 1996 letter to you proves you are a good man who kept his word. What a powerful love story!

I encourage you to get the book published. It would be a benefit to any soldier, soldier's wife, and anyone facing obstacles in life. It would also be refreshing to put something good out in this troubled world. Something that proves that a young black man can be strong, courageous, faithful, and full of love and a sense of duty.

Deacon Wright, excellent movies like "Hacksaw Ridge" started just like this, with one man telling his war story. Be encouraged.

Your Sister in Christ,
Sara L. Green

Table of Contents

Acknowledgements

Special thanks to my wife Gina for her understanding, patience and support.

Thanks to my sister-in-law Sylvia, who experienced the times of the book and maintained an active interest as a resource and encouraged me in the writing.

To my sister Joyce, thanks for your encouragement and support.

To my brother Michael, thanks for your advice and support.

To Diane Browne and Kris Hillman, thanks for your encouragement and support.

Thanks to my relentless editor and friend Nate Jones for your assistance and support.

Thanks to my niece Kathryn (K.D.) for the inspirational music from the "70's and 80's".

Special thanks to Sara Green for her review and encouragement.

Introduction

On Wednesday July 21, 1971, I arrived at the
Indianapolis Airport around three o'clock in the afternoon.
I had just completed my two years of active duty in the
United States Army. I was wearing my dressed green
uniform adorned with all the ribbons and badges that
represented all my military awards and accommodations.
Personally, I thought I looked very impressive. When I
deplaned, I was expecting an exuberant welcome from my
mom and fiancée, but I was also expecting some response
of gratitude from the crowd recognizing my service to the
country. My mom and fiancée fulfilled my expectations,
but I was surprised at the reaction from the crowd. There
were looks of disdain and no acknowledgements of
gratitude from a grateful nation.

That evening I was at home listening to the six
o'clock news hoping to pick up some current info on the
War. I did hear information on how the War was
progressing, but what I also heard was a lot of negative
things being said about the soldiers who were returning
from the War. I was blown away; we were not all murders,
baby killers, drug addicts or mental and emotional wrecks.
Most of us came back mature, disciplined adults ready to
be productive members of society. We had been trained to
be leaders, team players, productive, and mission focused.

Later on, that evening I went to my fiancée's house
(Barbara) and we talked about what I had heard on the
news. She informed me that what I heard was the sentiment
of most of the people and that it was even more prevalent
on college and university campuses. America was tired of

the War. I was shocked and hurt. I was looking forward to wearing my uniform for the next few days, especially to Church that Sunday. However, as a result of what I had just heard I took my uniform, packed it in a protective garment bag and never initiated conversation on the Vietnam War or my participation in it for the next forty years. It wasn't until Desert Storm when our country had a more favorable view of service men and women that the country started to see the Combat Soldier as a Hero.

During those forty years, on various occasions those who found out about my service record and participation in the Vietnam War would always ask me how did I make it. What they were really asking was why didn't I get hooked on drugs or why wasn't I emotionally unstable or how did I become a successful and productive member of society when other Vietnam Veterans didn't. During those times, I really did not have a viable concrete answer to give. Years went by before I could answer those questions. And to be truthful, I don't think you could give one generic reason that would apply to all Veterans. The war affected us all, but in different ways. The issues and challenges we faced after the War were often the result of our actions during the War.

On Saturday, June 3rd (2017) I was cleaning out my garage when I noticed under my work bench a green plastic container. When I pulled it out from beneath the bench I recognized what it was. The container belonged to my first wife Barbara who died in 2002. I opened the container and it was full of letters and cards that I had written to her during my two years in Military Service. For the next week, I took my time and sorted and arranged each letter in chronological order. There were over 120 letters. About 90% were in good condition and the rest were in fair

3

condition. Over the next few days I read each letter and some twice. It was a very emotional time for me because it brought back a lot of memories about the War and my fiancée who became my wife of thirty-one years. But more importantly within the letters was the answer that explained how I "made it", especially during my tour of duty in the Vietnam War.

One of the controversies/arguments that plagued the Vietnam War was, was it an all-out war or was it just a military conflict. Well, for those of us who were there, there is no doubt in our minds that was a "war". Soldiers were wounded, disabled, and dying in battle. That's a War! After reading the letters I saw the war as both. At the age of twenty I viewed it as a War with many conflicts. The conflicts that I personally faced were: (1) The North Vietnamese Army and the Viet Cong Guerrillas. (2) The loneliness of separation; will my fiancée and I be able to overcome loneliness and temptation and remain faithful to one another during this period of separation. (3) Fear and doubt; was my faith in God strong enough to overcome the fear of death by doubting God's promise of deliverance.

I then realized that in order to survive this "war" I would have to address each conflict differently. My M-16 Rifle and other Military Weapons would prove to be effective against the enemy, but not against the loneliness of separation nor fear and doubt. So, I came up with two more weapons to effectively address all three conflicts. To effectively deal with loneliness of separation I had to communicate, communicate, and communicate. And my weapon would be Pen, Paper, and Pictures (lots of letters). I figured that with letters and pictures I would keep Barb's memories of me and my love for her fresh in her heart and mind. To effectively address faith, we both had to pray

4

without ceasing. It would be through prayer that we would remain together spiritually. We've always believed that our relationship was a match made in heaven.

So, to answer that question, "How did I make it through the Vietnam War whole?" Well, when you finish reading these letters you can see how I took a holistic approach. I identified my enemies and used the right weapon to ensure a total victory. As a result, I left the Vietnam War "Physically, Emotionally, and Spiritually Whole."

"Weapons of War" has given me the opportunity to tell my Vietnam story and how it affected me, my fiancée, and my family. It will give my family a written record of my service to my country. And to thank the United States Army for its role in shaping my character and developing me into a responsible leader ready and equipped to take on any challenge or mission. In other words, helping me to "be all that I can be". And to finally tell my story of how the Army took a "Raw Recruit" and turned him into a trained Combat Soldier and proven Leader.

Note: I sincerely believe that if every able-bodied person were required to spend at least two years in a branch of the Armed Services of the United States they would benefit themselves and their nation. We would have better leaders, fathers, mothers, and more responsible, disciplined, and productive men and women taking their place in society.

Bob & Bob "1968"

Barbara A. Hampton   Robert E. Wright

Bobbie   Bobby

Bob Jr.   Bob Sr.

I am my beloved's, and my beloved is mine.

Song 6.3

In the heart, a man plans his course, but the Lord determines his steps.

Section 1: Basic Training

Fort Knox, Kentucky

22 Jul 1969
Dear Bob Jr,

How are you doing? I know you're having a tough time. Last night, when we said goodbye to each other I never felt so bad. Bob, I really love you. I guess I kind of took our love for granted because we were always together. But now that we are separated for the first time all I can say is "the next two years are going to be tough." I'm glad you called the house this morning before I left. But on the other hand, I couldn't stand to hear you cry. I'm going to do all I can to keep us together. I know what you'll be saying when you get this letter. You're going to try and be strong and reassure me and yourself how strong our love is for each other. I have no doubt that it is, but I have a hunch we are going to be tested. Bob, I promise that I'll do everything that is humanly possible to stay in touch with you. If I have to I'll write you every day to constantly remind you of our love for each other. Mom had a hard time too this morning. Promise me that you'll stay as close to her as you can. She knows how I feel about you and she realizes the impact you've had on my life. Before I met you, mom thought she was going to lose me to the streets. But you saved me Bob. You gave me hope and made me feel like I could make something of myself.

Well, Mr. D dropped me off at the Armed Services Reception Center about 5:45 A.M. And guess what, Mr. D gave me a sack and told me Mom wanted to make sure I took it with me. Bob, I looked in the bag and there were two peanut butter and jelly  *sandwiches and I started crying. My mom has always loved us like that. Please look in on her from time to time.*

At the Armed Services Center they gave us full medical exams and we swore an oath to defend and protect the United States of America. A couple of hours later we were herded onto buses headed for Fort Knox, Kentucky. It was a very lonely ride. We didn't know each other nor did we know what was in store for us. We felt like animals headed for the slaughter. It was about 2:30 in the afternoon and they hadn't fed us anything. Most of the inductees brought snacks out of the vending machines before we left Indianapolis. Of course, when I pulled out my peanut butter and jelly sandwiches I felt like I was being stalked by vultures.

Bob, we finally arrived at Fort Knox around 4:30 P.M. We were assigned to our units and we march/walked to our assigned barracks. We were told to put our gear on our bunks and report outside "on the double". Bob, my first day at Basic Training was humiliating. All throughout grade school, Jr. High, and High School when lining up for any activity I was always last because they always went in alphabetical order. Since my last name started with a "W" of course I was last all the time. But in the Army, they do things differently. They go by alphabetical order but they start not at the front with "A" but from the back with "Z". Our barracks was the first in line to go through the Mess Hall for chow. So, they needed five people for KP (kitchen

police) for the evening chow period which meant feeding the whole Battalion (1,000 inductees). So, guess who was one of those chosen, yours truly. We had to serve everybody else before we could eat.

Then after we ate we had to clean pots, pans, dishes, floors, just about everything. Bob, we even had to setup up the Mess Hall for breakfast tomorrow morning. Just think this has to be done three times a day. I was worn out just taking the garbage out. Bob, when we were done it was 11:00 P.M. and we had to get up at 5 A.M. Now I understand that little cliché, "You're in the Army now." That means life as we knew it is over!

Well, Bob, I need to get some sleep. Writing this letter was hard. If it wasn't for my bunk being close to the fire light I couldn't have done it. We don't even have access to writing paper yet. As you can see I wrote this one on the back of fliers. I hope it will fit in the envelope. I'll get you my mailing address as soon as I can. I can't tell you how much I miss you and how much I love you. Be strong because, getting through the next two years is going to take all the love that we have for each other.

Love,
Robt.

Basic Training

23 Jul 1969

Dear Bob Jr,

Bob, how are you feeling today? A little better I hope. The one advantage that I have is our days are long and hectic. Today we got up at 5AM again and started out spending one hour learning the Army's way to make up a bed. The covers have to be so tight that you should be able to drop a dime on them and it bounces. And until all beds are that tight nobody eats breakfast. I was surprised how comfortable the mattress is. You can really get

a good night's sleep. After all the bunks passed inspection, we did one hour of PT (Physical Training) then we finally went to breakfast.

After breakfast, we went to the Parade field to learn how to march. The assistant Drill Sergeant was amazed at how quick I was catching on. Bob, I have not told them yet that I had two semesters of ROTC in High School. I guess I must have impressed our Drill Sergeant because he asked me to take the five worst marchers off to the side and work with them individually. Bob, I worked with them for two hours straight. You wouldn't believe it but their main problem was they did not know their right from their left. So, I asked them what hand did they write with. They all raised their right hand; that was perfect. I then told them if the command is "right face" then pivot on the foot that's on the opposite side of your writing hand. That worked in theory but we still had to work on it awhile. After two hours, they were able to execute a "right face" a "left face" and "about face." We rejoined the rest of the unit and we marched for another two hours. When we got back to the barracks our Drill Sergeant said to me, "I don't want to know how you did it but it shows you have some leadership ability." That's when I told him about my ROTC experience. He said that he would keep that in mind.

Well, I'm bushed. I'm going to get this letter to the mail box, take a shower, and hit the sack. I'll stare at your picture until they turn the lights out. I'm on the bottom bunk so when I get in my bunk I put your senior picture in the springs of the bunk above me. I look at your picture for awhile and then I flip it over and read the words, "love always", until I fall asleep.

Love,
Robt.

Basic Training

25 Jul 1969
Dear Bob Jr,

Today is Friday and my third letter of the week. Bob, I know "absence makes the heart grow fonder" and please forgive me for saying "and absence will also cause the heart to wonder". Bob, I know you love me dearly, but it's because I love you so much that I'm not taking any chances of losing you. So right now, I'm declaring war on what I call "the loneliness of separation". And my weapon will be pen and paper. Regardless of where I am or what situation I'm in I'm going to write you as much as I can. Over the next two years there's at least one thing you'll find out about me and that's how much you mean to me. My goal is to keep in touch, keep you lifted up, and always, always let you know how much I love you, miss you, and need you. Bob I'm going to write to you so much that you are going to know how I think, why, and who (you) I'm thinking about.

This will probably be the First Friday we haven't been together in over four years. Your mother won't know what to think. I remember the time we were out on the front porch and when she came out she asked me, "Robert, don't you have a home?" Then she told me if I keep hanging around all the time she was going to start charging me rent. You know, I assumed she was kidding but if she wasn't I would have paid it. You are worth it. When I started working for the Telephone Company and bought my own car (Chevy Biscayne 3-speed), on Fridays we were gone so much that the only time she saw me was when I picked you up and when I dropped you off. And the only reason she saw me then was because I respected you and her enough to come up to the house and get you. Plus, you always greeted me as if your "Prince Charming" had just arrived. And guess what, I was ready to whisk you off to the palace. But since we weren't married yet I couldn't do that.

So, in the meantime it will be awhile before I can whisk you off again, but there will come a day when I won't have to bring you back, because you will be at the Palace with your "Prince" (me). I hope you have a good day. My letters should arrive any day now. I miss you, Bob.

Love,

Robt.

Basic Training
27 Jul 1969
Dear Bob Jr,

How's my Bob Jr. doing today? Did you go to Church? I hope so. You know one of our" Weapons of War" is "faith". Bob, I think God is going to do something

12

special with us so we have to be plugged in to him. We don't want to get outside of his will. I think the journey we're about to take will be a testimony someday. I got up

early, went to chow and made it to Chapel Service. We have pretty much the day off. I'm going to try and call you today. It will depend on whether or not I can get access to a phone (guys stay lined up all day to get to a phone) and catching you at home. I know if I call you and you're not home you'll be very upset.

Well, Babe, I'm going to get to the PX, I'll try the phones later. I hope you have received at least one of my letters by now. I think it will help you feel a little better.

Love,
Robt.

Basic Training

30 Jul 1969
Dear Bob Jr,
How are you doing today? I'm sorry I haven't had a chance to write in the past two days. We've been going from 5A.M. to 8P.M. the last few days. It hasn't been too bad. During the day we do PT, Marching, and attend classes on everything from first aid to what to do in the

*event of a chemical attack. After the chemical attack class
we actually go through a gas chamber and take off our gas
masks so we can feel the effects of C.S. gas. It's not pretty
when we come out but for the rest of the day your sinuses
are clear. After evening chow, we have another two-hour
class and that ended our day around 8P.M.*

*Bob guess what! I've been selected by my Drill
Sergeant to be a "Squad Leader". That means, I'm
responsible for providing leadership to eight trainees. Are
you proud of me? It doesn't change my rank or anything
like that but I do get a few privileges that the other trainees
won't get. Plus, I'll be wearing a Leadership armband (two
strips). I guess the real benefit will be the development of
my leadership skills and the ability to assume
responsibility. Bob, the one thing we do consistently is
"march". We march on long hikes, we march to our
classes, we march everywhere we go. The marching helps
to develop our cohesiveness as a unit. We say Marching
Chants like, "Grab your rifle and follow me, I am the
Infantry" or "Ain't no use in going home, Jody's got your
girl and gone." By the way, when I come home on my first
three day pass you and I will have to have a long talk about
the potential Jody's that will surely be coming your way.*

*Now for the best part, I got some of your letters and
pictures yesterday. First of all, Melvin takes better pictures
than Sylvia. So, stick with Mel. And don't tell Sylvia I said
that, because she'll find some way to torture me. Bob, your
letters said just what I wanted to hear. That you love me
more than anything else in the world. As a matter of fact,
you said it several times (smile). And I'm glad my letters
brought you comfort too. Now when we get lonely for each
other we'll at least have our letters to go back to read and
re-read and re-read (laugh). Bob, I love you and miss you*

so much. I'm so sorry you have to go through this. This separation is not going to be easy, but I know our love for each other is strong enough to get us through. Bob for the next two years our motto will be to "Stay Focused on the Future." And the future is us getting married and raising a family. That's been our goal for the past four years. And two years is nothing in comparison to a lifetime. Bob in your pictures I see a big box of "Kleenex". Maybe if I write a few more letters you won't need the Kleenex, or maybe we can get it down to a smaller box (smile). All jokes aside, I know how you're feeling. Believe me I feel the same. I'm just trying to be strong for the both of us. But I'll be honest with you, at times I have my moments too. You are so precious to me and I love you so very much. Stay strong and stay "focused".

Love,
Robt.

Tell everybody I said HI! And tell your Mother I miss her.

Basic Training
02 Aug 1969
Dear Bob Jr,

Yesterday was a busy day for me. First, I received two passionate letters from you that I will cherish and read over and over and over. Those letters really touched my heart. You assured me of your love for me and your commitment to our relationship as we go through this period of separation. Bob, I really needed to hear that, not because I had any doubts, but because it reassures me that you'll be with me all the way.

15

Yesterday, we were shown a movie on the effectiveness of weapons used by the U.S. Army in previous and current wars. As I watched the movie it became very clear to me that I could or probably will be sent to Vietnam; subsequently be put in a life or death situation. Last night, as I was lying on my bunk I looked up and saw your picture in the bed springs above me and fear and doubt overcame me I started thinking about the possibility of my not surviving the war, and more specifically what would happen to you. Bob, the thought of it was so horrible that I relied on my faith and just started praying. I fell off to sleep and had this wonderful dream of us being married and raising our children. When I woke up this morning I realized that from time to time I'll have those feelings. But I also realized that the best weapon against fear and doubt is "faith" in God and in his promises. So, Bob, you keep writing those letters. I truly believe God has a plan for us that exceeds well past the Vietnam War.

Secondly, yesterday we received our M-14 Rifles. We spent all day learning the different parts; we took them apart, cleaned them, and put the rifle back together. We learned how to do parade movements with them and we spent about an hour and a half marching with them. The only thing I didn't agree with was when our Drill Sergeant said that we should love our rifles more than we should love our girlfriends and wives. I get all that about it saving lives and everything, but Bob I'll only need my rifle for the next two years. I'll need and depend on you for a lifetime.

Bob, we normally have training on Saturday for half a day. But today after training we had to start preparing for next Wednesday's GI inspection. That's an inspection where everything in the barracks has to squeaky clean and in order. Including ourselves. So, we're going to spend this afternoon and learn how to spit-shine our spare pair of boots. If we don't pass inspection as a unit we won't get our two-day pass next week. Bob, as I watched our Drill Sergeant demonstrate how to spit-shine a pair of boots I just watched and kept my  *mouth shut. When he finished I started working on my boots and when I finished I had every mouth in the barracks hanging wide open. You see Bob, I never told anyone that I shined shoes on Indiana Avenue for three years during High School. So, I spent three hours helping groups of threes learn my process. I was determined that if we didn't pass inspection next week it won't be for un-shined boots. They won't look like Stacy-Adams, but I can guarantee that if the sun is shining you won't have to look up to see it.*

Now do you realize how much I love you, Bob. I'll do whatever it takes to see you, even if it means repositioning the Sun (laugh).

Love,
Robt.

03 Aug – 10 Aug 69

No Letters Found for This Period

Basic Training
11 Aug 1969
Dear Bob Jr,
*Bob when I
returned to the barracks
last night I just couldn't
stop thinking about you.
Being home with you
this weekend on a two-day pass was wonderful. I think we
tried to make up for two and a half weeks in 48 hours. We
had so much fun together in just 48-hours I can only
imagine what a life together as man and wife will be like. I
was a little self-conscious when I first saw you because I
didn't know how you would like me without my mustache
and with my GI haircut. I know you've seen me in pictures
but this was up front and personal. When I asked you about
it I'll never forget what you said. You just grabbed me and
gave me a gentile kiss and said, "As long as your kiss
hadn't changed I didn't care." You then told me that I was
your handsome soldier and that you'll take me any way you
can. I still thought that I looked like a nerd.*

*Bob, for the next twenty-three-months this is what our
lives are going to be like; me going and coming and long
periods of separation in between. We're really going to
have to stay in constant communication with each other in
order to combat the loneliness and temptations that we're
going to have to endure. In about three weeks you'll be
heading back to school and will be faced with many
challenges. And I'm not just talking about academics.*

Initially you'll be strong and able to resist. But as time wears on, loneliness and separation will tear at your heart, which will eventually affect a change in your emotions and feelings and finally your judgment will be clouded. The best way we can keep this scenario from developing is again by "communicating" with each other. We'll have to be open and honest with each other and share anything that could have an impact on our relationship.

 *Bob, for the next six weeks our training will be very intense. The focus will be on developing us into combat soldiers. We will be trained on every weapon at our disposal. Even hand-to-hand combat (tell Sylvia "no," I will not teach her H-T-H-C). Plus, I'm restricted to the base so I won't have the time or the opportunity to deal with the distractions you'll have to face. But after a year of working out in the public as a Telephone Installer I've had a few distractions that I had to deal with. Not only have I learned how to deal with them but also how to avoid them. Bob, when I left you last night I was totally aware of the precious jewel that I was leaving behind. You are a very valuable treasure that I have found, and do not intend to lose.*

Love,
Robt.

12 Aug – 17 Sep 69
No Letters Found for This Period

Basic Training
18 Sept 1969-1
Dear Bob Jr,

What are you up to these days? I know you still love me, because I still love you very much. I miss you so much. My life feels so empty without you. I need someone to hold, kiss, and love. And you're the only one that can meet those needs for me. Bob, I really like the pictures you sent in your last letter. I wish I could keep them but I'd rather you keep them for us.

Well, we have eight more days until graduation and I'm glad. I'm ready for my next assignment. I know we're still training, but it feels like we're in more of a waiting mode. And it's driving me nuts. I wish you were here. I think what's really driving me nuts is being without you. Well, they're signaling for chow now so I'd better end this letter now. I'll write you again later.

Love,
Robt.

Basic Training

18 Sept 1969 - 2

Dear B0b Jr,

I just wanted to take time out and remind you of how much I love you and miss you. I love you so much that it's mind boggling. My days start and end with you on my mind. During the day I think about you, at night I dream about you, and in between I write you letters. Don't worry I'm not walking around like a lovesick Zombie. I still stay focused on my training. My main focus is to survive and then come back home and marry you.

Bob some people have told me that the Army will make a man out of me. Well, I believe a good woman can do that too. Growing up in the "hood" and then meeting a super smart and lovely girl like you I knew I had to up my game. I knew you were going to finish high school, and go on to College and be successful so I knew I had to change. I was determined to be whatever it would take for you to fall in love with me. So, I decided to work on being the man that you would want and deserve. Since the summer of 1965 I have devoted my heart and soul trying to develop into that man. You were my motivation for change. So, since you got me this far I guess God decided to use Uncle Sam to finish the job. I just don't like the fact that separation (from you) is now part of my development process. But I know that over the next two years through separation not only will I come back to you a better man, our love for each other will be tested and become a lot stronger than it was before I left (Absence makes the heart grow fonder).

Bob, I love you very much. As far as I'm concerned other than God Almighty life begins and ends with you. Well, it's getting kind of late and I must say goodnight.

*Again, I love you and when I get out of the service I'm going to make you my wife, "**Just You Wait and See.**"*

Love,
Robt.

Basic Training
21 Sept 1969
Dear Bob Jr,
Five more days and Basic Training will be history. One down three to go.

Bob, how are you? Have you been a good girl? I hope you liked the pictures I sent you. I feel bad because I can't give you anything for your birthday. But I'll try to find something not too expensive.

Bob, it will be awhile before I'll be able to call you. By the way, a guy in my platoon said he saw my orders. He said that I was going to Fort Ord in California. They have three schools there; Infantry, Cooks, and Administrative Clerks. But you can't go by rumors in the Army. I'll just wait until Monday then I'll know for sure where my next stop will be. But no matter where they send me, it's not far enough to diminish my love for you. It will reach you from wherever I am.

Well, sorry, I've got to go. We're getting ready to study for our C – 41 Test. Be good and remember that I love you very much. As long as I live you'll always be mine and I'll always be yours.

Love,
Robt.

Basic Training

22 Sept 1969 - 1

Dear Bob Jr,

Well, it's all over. Today we took the C – 41 Test. And I did not do as well as I would have liked. Out of a possible 67 points I scored 63. That was good enough to rank fifth in the Company (200 men). Thank God for two semesters of ROTC at Attucks.

Now, for the bad news. We got our orders today and my next assignment is Advance Infantry Training at Fort Polk, Louisiana. That is Infantry and jungle fighting school. Bob, when I heard that I was really upset. I was going to call you tonight but I won't. I would have sounded so pitiful I probably would have made you cry. So, I'll just have my own pity party and get over it. We'll be leaving for Fort Polk Saturday so I won't be home this weekend. We probably won't see each other for about two and a half months. Then we'll probably get a fourteen-day pass before our next assignment, which for most of us will probably be the Republic of South Vietnam.

Bob, before I end this letter I want to say, "I love you very much." No matter what happens my love will only be for you and you only. You have made life so meaningful and enjoyable for me. My life has been so different since we've been together. And to think these past few years will only be a sample of what life will be like when we get married. If I feel better tomorrow I'll call you, but I won't promise. I just feel so dejected. I just want to be alone for a few days to think things out. But don't worry I won't shut you out. You're the main reason I've got to think. The one thing that is on my mind is whether or not I should give you the ring for Christmas. Should I saddle you with an engagement ring knowing that I could be in combat in two and a half months? Is that fair to you?

I've got to go. I'm really getting depressed now! I love you with all my heart.

P.S. Happy Birthday!!!

Love,
Robt.

Basic Training
22 Sept 1969 - 2
Dear Bob Jr,

I've made my decision. No matter where they send me, I'm going to put a ring on your finger. Bob, I love you and I know you love me, now I want to proclaim it to the world. Together, life will be wonderful, especially when the baby arrives in "72". I know you will be a wonderful wife and mother. I can't wait to see you dressed in white standing next to me at the altar. I can feel the first kiss of our new life as man and wife. Your lips will be as soft as always. We'll be holding each other so tight the Minister will have to pry us apart.

Well, now that I've got that decision off my chest I'm going to get ready to go to bed. It's past midnight and I'll probably be up half the night thinking about the conflict across the big pond (Vietnam). So, babe, be happy and remember we'll be together again soon.

Love,
Robt.

Basic Training
24 Sept 1969
Dear Bob Jr,

How is my one and only love doing these days? I didn't receive a letter from you today. But I'm not worried because tomorrow I'll probably get two; I hope, I hope, I hope. Besides I realize you didn't attend Ball State just to write me letters. But between your studies, cheerleading, and socializing (sorority events and dances) keep the letters coming. Bob, I'm so sorry I won't be there with you on

your birthday. This will be the first one that I'll miss in the four years we've been together. Oh, you know what, it just came to mind that I told you to stop writing while in transition to Fort Polk. So never mind my second statement in this letter. Although you can go ahead and write the letters, just hold on to them until I send you my new address and then you can send them all at once (smile).

Well, today we had our last class in character guidance. The subject was "Sex, Marriage, and the Soldier." It was very interesting. The Chaplain made us remember three words, "Sex is Sacred." And the only time you have the right to have sex is in marriage. Bob, he made a lot of sense especially to a bunch of soldiers away from home. He also planted a good seed for those who are fortunate enough to return home. Bob, that means you're going to have to be awfully strong when I get home. I get the message though; although sex is a part of the love relationship the proper time to have it is after marriage and with "your" spouse. Bob, again I say when I get home <u>you're</u> *going to have to be very strong, for both of us.*

Bob, because of you I have so much to live for. But in a few months, I'll be surrounded by death. Even though it must be God's will for me I'm concerned it's a threat to our future together. So, we must be very diligent about our prayer life. And pray to God that he keeps me from harm's way and return me home in one piece. Also, that he keeps you from harm's way (wolves). You are a very lovely and desirable young lady and I can't protect you from here, but I trust you very much.

I've got to go but I won't stop and put my pen down until I say, "I love you and I miss you very much.

Love,
Robt.

Basic Training

25 Sept 1969
Dear Bob Jr,
How are you doing? I guess I'm doing pretty good. We graduate tomorrow and from here you know where I'll

 *be headed. We're supposed to go by plane and I'm scared to death (first plane ride). It was kind of cold today and I almost froze when I got up this morning. Bob, yesterday I was looking at the September Playboy Magazine and the playmate in the centerfold favored you so much I had to keep it (I'm sure you understand). Her body and your body are almost identical.*

Bob, in this letter I'm going to send you my certificate of promotion. Please take good care of it for me. It means a lot to both of us. It recognizes my military achievements and the first time we've been separated for an extended period of time.

Well, I've got to go. I love you very much. Don't study too hard, and don't forget me.

Love,
Robt.

Basic Training

26 Sept 1969
Dear Bob Jr,

How are you doing? I want you to know how excited I was to see you and mom at my graduation today. That was a real emotional moment for me. I didn't think anyone would be able to show up. And then to look up and see the two most important women in your life. "Wow!" I only

wish you and I could have had a little time alone. But I was so happy anyway. I love you both so much!

After the two of you left I went over to the day room and watched T.V. Those were the saddest moments of my life. After a while I fell asleep and when I woke up it was almost 6:00 P.M. I'm still a little leery about riding in an airplane. I'm going to try and write you a letter on the plane.

Bob, after I saw you today I was again reminded of how much I really do love you. You're so pretty and loving;

this next two and a half months are really going to be a challenge for me. When you left with Mom, I would have given anything to have climbed in the car and drove off with you. This morning I woke up looking forward to a day with myself and your letters, but God had something in store that was a whole lot better. My mom and my future wife. Well, I got to go, as it's 9PM. Love you soooooooo much. Pray for me tomorrow.

Love,
Robt.

Section 2:

Advanced Infantry Training

Fort Polk, Louisiana

27 Sept 1969
Dear Bob Jr,
How are things going? Did you have a nice birthday?
I wish I could have been there with you. I miss you so
much.

Let me tell you about my first plane trip. Bob, it was
something else. When we reached cruising altitude and
leveled off I finally opened my eyes. And I never saw
anything more beautiful in my life. Deep blue sky and big
fluffy white clouds! The flight was relatively smooth. I
really enjoyed the flight until we started to descend. Then it
felt as if my body was being attacked. My ears were
stopped up and everything from my neck down started
hurting. And that's not the worse part. When we got off the
airplane it was like walking into a huge furnace. It was
about 95 degrees. Fort Polk is about 17 miles from the
Texas border.

Bob, it is rough down here at Fort Polk. I hope I can
get my M.O.S. changed, so I can get out of the Infantry. For
example, everywhere we go we have to run. And every time
your right foot touches the ground you have to holler
"Kill." Our Platoon Sergeant informed us that for the next
two and a half months the Army is going to train us on who
to kill, how to kill, and when to kill, period! Bob, I'm not a
killer, I'm a lover (smile).

Bob, guess what? I've got poison ivy again. Don't laugh, it ain't funny. My face and neck are covered with it. Between the plane landing, all the killing and the poison ivy I'm pretty miserable right now. But you know I really shouldn't be complaining about poison ivy. It was poison ivy that brought us together in the first place. If you remember in the summer of "65" we and some of the other neighborhood kids were on a bus on our way to spend the day at one of the State Parks in southern Indiana. At that time, I had poison ivy all over my arms. And at that time, I was new to the neighborhood so nobody cared to sit next to the new kid who had poison ivy. Nobody but you Bob. You came over and sat next to me the entire trip to the park and the entire trip coming back from the park. At that moment, I asked myself who is this kind, considerate, and very cute girl. And believe me I was determined to find out. And we spent the rest of the summer getting to know one another. When we went back to school for the fall semester it was no secret about our relationship because our identities changed from Robert E. Wright and Barbara A. Hampton to Bob & Bob.

I hate to say this but I don't know if seeing you Friday helped me or hurt me. I didn't get to touch you or hold you enough. We didn't even get an opportunity for a good kiss. We got a peck in but we're not birds. We're two human beings who love each other very much. We didn't have a chance to express our love towards each other deeply. Now we'll have to wait two and a half months.

Bob, please don't write me until I let you know. I'm still trying to change my M.O.S. and they won't let us keep more than three letters at a time. So, I need to figure out our mailing intervals. I cherish your letters almost as much as I cherish you. So, I don't want anyone to have any excuse for monitoring my mail. Got to go. I'll write you in a couple of days. I hope one of these days I can show you how deep my love is for you. I love you yesterday, today and forever.

Love,
Robt.

Advanced Infantry Training

29 Sept 1969
Dear Bob Jr,

What have you been doing lately? I've tried everything possible to get out of here but I was unsuccessful. Now I can focus on training so I can develop the skills I'll need to survive this war.

After being here a couple of days, I've had a chance to see and hear some of the horrible things that are actually happening in South Vietnam. And I've come to the conclusion that if our children are going to grow up in a free society then I have to do what I can to stop communist aggression. In addition, what I'm going to experience over the coming months will be essential for my development in the areas of responsibility, commitment, integrity, and devotion. In other words when I left you I was a young man and when I return I'll return as a more mature man. Understanding the responsibility of having a family, the commitment to caring for and protecting my family, being a devoted father and husband, and having the type of character that others will respect and honor. And most of all, being thankful to God for delivering me from danger and watching over you.

After saying all that, "no," I haven't been brain washed by the Army. And, "no," I haven't become a crusader. But I do realize that part of the maturing process is overcoming obstacles. And Bob, you too will have some obstacles you'll have to overcome while I'm in Vietnam and while you're at Ball State. How we overcome will have an impact on our future together. The obstacles that I have to face soon will be the North Vietnamese Regular Army and the Viet Cong. So, I'm going to stay focused on the things I need to do to overcome my obstacles. Learn everything I can here at Fort Polk so I'll be trained and equipped to face and overcome my obstacles. My determination to overcome my obstacles is determined by my objective. And my objective is to get back home and marry you. And I am determined, motivated and focused on making that happen. Thinking of you always, I love you very much.

Love,
Robt.

Advanced Infantry Training
30 Sept 1969
Dear Bob Jr,
How is life back there in "civilization?" It's miserable here. In the last two days, they have started treating us like dogs. From the time I got here I had to go three days before anyone did anything about my poison ivy. Bob, if you could see me now you won't recognize me. My face is covered with the stuff.

Today we went to the field and learned how to disassemble, assemble and fire the 45-caliber pistol.

32

Bob, I don't know if I'm going to make it or not. But I'm trying very hard. This weather down here is HOT! It's 90 degrees every day. And with all this poison ivy on my face I feel like I have a very uncomfortable mask on. If I were home right now the only thing that I would want masking my face would be your soft kisses.

You can start writing me now. But no more than two letters a week. Bob, for the next two months you're going to have to be happy for both of us. I know that's an unusual request but it will help. You know what, I've figured it out. Suffering and being miserable is part of our training.

I have to go. But I'm not going anywhere until I tell you how much I love you, how much I miss you and how much I want to hold you-----A WHOLE LOT!!

Love,
Robt.

Advanced Infantry Training
2 Oct 1969
Dear Bob Jr.,
How is my future wife doing? Is everything going well at school? Today we learned how to operate the M-79 Grenade Launcher. It fires a shell that has the same explosive power as a regular hand grenade, (a killing radius of fifteen meters). However, it's more effective than a hand grenade because the grenade round is shot from a launcher rather than thrown with your hand. It's more accurate and you can aim and shoot at greater distances

*than pulling a pin and
throwing it, especially
when you're under enemy
fire.*

*Last night for movie
night they showed an old
John Wayne war movie.
During the movie, my
mind began to wonder
and I remember the last
time we were at a drive-
in movie together. It was a week before I was to report for
service. We made it through the first feature and the
intermission, but during the second feature we did
something we had never done before. We had a long talk
about our future. Do you remember that? You were very
talkative. We talked about being separated for two years
and how painful that was going to be. We talked about
getting married when I get out of the Service and how many
children we will have. We talked about our love for each
other and how we'll miss each other. Then when we finish
talking we sat there quietly for a while as I held you in my
arms. Then after about a half hour you raised your head up
and with tears in your eyes and gave me a very soft tender
kiss and said, "Robert, I love you very much and I always
will." And if you remember I kissed you softly and said to
you that "I've been in love with you since the first day I met
you." I just didn't think I was good enough for you. Then
we left for home. I drove with one hand on the wheel and
the other hand was holding your hand. Bob, I don't think
I'll ever forget that night at the Lafayette Square Drive-in.*

*Bob, I probably won't see you again until December.
We'll only get two (2-day) weekend passes for the whole*

time we're at Fort Polk. So, I'll probably spend my time on base. I'll stay out of trouble that way. This weather down here is crazy. In the mornings, it's so cool and pleasant, but around 10 A.M. you can start feeling the heat, then the rest of the day it's murder.

Bob, I don't think I'll be doing as well down here as I did in Basic Training. Because most of the guys down here are big and husky. It's like they weeded out all the weaklings in Basic Training.

Well, I have to go. I know it's only the 1st of October I can't wait to see you in December. It will undoubtedly be too cold for the drive-in but I'm sure we'll find someplace warm. You'll be in charge of self-control. I love you very much.

Love,
Robt.

Advanced Infantry Training

4 Oct 1969 - 1
Dear Bob Jr,

I just came back from church. I hope you have received some of my letters by now. I can't wait to get one from you.

Bob, this is October and it's still "HOT" down here. The temperature reaches between 89 and 93 degrees every day. And they keep us going every day, ALL DAY! We don't complain much because we understand the more fit we are and the more combat ready we are the better our chances to stay alive.

Bob, yesterday we went to a weapons demonstration. Just before the demonstration began they played a record. On the record was the song of the infantryman. The title of the song was "Come and Follow Me". I thought that was an appropriate title because the infantryman is normally the first soldier to engage the enemy. His job is to identify and remove any obstacle that poses a threat to those that follow him. Bob, that's who I want to be in life, "Your (infantry) Man". I want to be the person that can confront and remove any obstacles that can endanger your hopes and dreams. And, I want you to "Follow Me" for life. A life of love, happiness, and togetherness. And I think you know that I am capable and willing to take on this mission. I know that we have already planned on getting married after I finish my active service obligations and after you finish college. But I wanted to take advantage of this military illustration to reassure you of my love for you and my commitment to you, and that fulfilling them both will be a lifelong mission.

Bob, my going to Vietnam is going to be a challenge for both of us. It's going to take prayer, love, and faith to get us through it. Prayer for God's protection and daily guidance. Love to maintain on a daily basis the bond we have between us. And faith, always trusting that God has put us together and that he has a future plan and purpose for us. My future happiness and success depends a lot on you being by my side. You're someone I want to hold onto for life.

Bob, I don't think I've ever said this to you, "I'm very proud of you." You're very smart, very attractive, and you have a very warm and sweet personality. And on top of all that, you are very talented. You are a very gifted singer. And I'm very proud of myself because out of all the suitors that have come your way you picked me. Now, I don't consider that as being lucky nor am I going to try and match attributes. You way over shadow me. I just consider

*it as divine favor. And God must have known there was
something in me that he would shape and develop to be a
suitable mate for you. So, I'll end by saying if you follow
me, I'll lead you in the way God will have us to go-------My
love for you will be the stage for your future.*

The Song of the Infantryman

*Oh Soldier, Oh Soldier, grab your rifle follow me. I
am the infantry. Wide river, wide river, River of Saigon one
more river to cross.*

*Bob, we only have one more river to cross before
we'll be together again.*

Love,
Robt.

Advanced Infantry Training
4 Oct 1969 - 2
Dear Bob Jr,

*Yes, it's me again. I guess we can call this a "two
letter-day." I just got back from Church. Yes, I even go to
Church at night. Tonight, at Church they showed some
movies about the lives of the children of Vietnam.
Particularly how the war has affected their lives. It's really
sad to see children who may never experience a normal
childhood or life. We saw what life was really like for them
over there. For example, we saw in this one movie how a
little Vietnamese boy had to watch as the Viet Cong
disemboweled his parents because they wouldn't allow his
older brother to join their army. Bob, it was horrible! The
little boy was so cute and innocent. Now he'll have to grow
up as an orphan in a war-torn community. However, the
Chaplain said that this little boy was saved by a 101st
Airborne unit who found him in the streets begging for food
and took him to an orphanage ran by American*

missionaries. But only one out of ten children end up so lucky. Then the Chaplain showed us another film that featured a little Vietnamese girl who walked into a Viet Cong booby trap and lost both her legs. It was a pitiful sight to see the expression on her face when the doctor's pulled back the sheets and she saw the bandages on her knees, and the rest of her legs were gone. She started crying and shouting in Vietnamese over and over again, "What happen to my legs, What happen to my legs." Believe me, Bob, it was bad enough watching all the suffering on a movie. I don't know how I'll handle it once I get over there and see it up front and personal. I know one thing, my personal feelings about going to Vietnam are changing. I'm not as angry about going as I used to be. Either the Army's indoctrination is working or maybe God is changing my heart so I can see things from his perspective rather than from my own, as a dangerous and unnecessary inconvenience on my life. Maybe it's his way of mentally and emotionally preparing me for the military role I'll have to play in Vietnam. Or, maybe God is using this experience as a way of making me a better man. After all, he is giving me one of his best daughters to love, cherish and care for. And Bob, from what I've seen so far I promise you this; our children will be loved, know Jesus and have the best education they can have. Even if we have to pay for it ourselves.

Well, I didn't mean to write all that. I started out wanting to tell you about the movies but I guess the Lord wanted me to reveal some other things. I'll close by reiterating how much I love you, how much I miss you and how much I cherish you.

Love,
Robt.

Angela A. Wright
Ball State University
College of Business
May 7, 1994

Nolise K. Wright
Ball State University
Teachers College
Dec. 16. 2001

"Debt Free"

"Debt Free"

Advanced Infantry Training

8 Oct 1969

Dear Bob Jr,

I miss your letters very much. But not as much as I miss you.

Bob, today was a sad day, someone was injured on the rifle range. Someone accidentally shot themselves in the foot with an M-16 rifle. The guys Platoon Leader said that the guy who had the accident will probably lose his foot. The bullet that is fired from an M-16 is a 7.62-millimeter round. When the bullet enters the body, it is designed to make a hole a little smaller than the size of a dime. But when it exits the body it leaves a hole the size of a silver dollar. The bullet travels at a speed of 3,725 meters a second. I'm glad the M-16 is our weapon and not theirs.

Bob, I went to church tonight and saw another nice movie. After the movie, the minister talked about people who are going through life without a goal or purpose. As I sat and listened I could only be thankful that was not my situation. I have a goal and purpose in my life. My goal is to marry you, have children and provide for the needs of my family. My purpose is the love I have for you and my devotion to you. As I said before, I think about you all the time. I pray for you every day. I pray for your safety, your success in school and yes, I'll admit it, I pray that your love for me will endure this period of separation. When I first told you that "I loved you" back in the summer of 1965 I'll admit I was very shy and insecure about my future. But every year since then as our relationship grew my shyness disappeared and my life took on a whole new focus. And Bob, you became my focus. And it was at that time that my life began to have meaning and purpose, "You".

P.S. *I'll try to call you soon. The Army is behind with our pay, again. I'm trying to scrape up some money to call you. Don't send me any. I'm going to try and stick this out until payday.*

Love,
Robt.

Advanced Infantry Training

9 Oct 1969
Dear Bob Jr,

What have you been doing lately? Besides thinking about me. How are you doing in your classes?

I was so happy to receive your letter yesterday. You said everything that I wanted to hear. Especially the ten times you said I love you. I'm so sorry they limited us to receive only two letters a week. But they never said how many pages they could be, "Hint," "Hint".

Well, life down here has gotten a little better. The weather has cooled off a little. But now it's raining cats and dogs. They say these all-day rains are similar to Monsoon season in Vietnam.

I have some good news for a change. Do you remember in basic training when I qualified for only a sharpshooter with the M-14 rifle? Well, today I qualified as an "expert" with the M-16. Now I'll have a sharpshooter and an expert Medal. Are you proud of me? Bob, I can't wait to come home on Thanksgiving. I know you're going to have a "BIG KISS" waiting for me. Anything will be better than the peck we had when you and mom came for my graduation from basic training. In addition to missing your kisses there is something else that I miss, your fried rib eye steaks. The chow down here is awful. But you dare not complain about it because the cooks will get an attitude quick.

I've got to go but again I want to let you know how much better I felt after receiving your letter. I can't survive without hearing from you. By the way my telephone money savings is building up. So, I'll probably be calling you next week. How does the first Wednesday after the 15th of each month sound for you. Let me know. Love you, miss you and I'm always thinking about you.

Love,
Robt.

Advanced Infantry Training

11 Oct 1969
Dear Bob Jr,

Bob, what are you doing on this nice Saturday? Thinking about me I hope. I want to tell you that in a few days you should receive a package from me. I'm not going to tell you what it is; I'll let it be a surprise.

"Write On"

Bob, I feel a lot better than I did when I first arrived at Fort Polk. Your two letters had a lot to do with it. Oh, big news! We learned today that the two letters a week mail restriction has been lifted. So anytime you get the urge, "Write On."

By the way, do you remember that incident when that guy accidentally shot himself in the foot with his M-16

Rifle? He's getting out of the Army on a medical discharge. But he paid dearly for it. They had to remove half his foot.

    I'm writing a little earlier today because we had only a half day of training. And it was mostly physical training (PT) and hand-to-hand combat. Sylvia would have enjoyed the hand-to-hand session. You know I remember when we use to sit on your porch and Sylvia would mess with you and you two would end up wrestling. But shortly after I started stopping by you quit fooling around like that. You started showing a lot less interest in fooling around with your sister and more interest in me. That had a boomerang effect because I started stopping by more. Then you started dressing different. You went from wearing jeans with holes in the knees and sweat shirts with half the sleeves cut off to nicer jeans and cute little sleeveless tops. You were transforming from a cute little tomboy to a very attractive, and I have to say "sexy young lady". Not only did I see the transformation, your mother saw it too. She started spending more time on the front porch too. But that was OK because the boomerang swung again. I got to spend more time chatting with your mother and when I told her how I was working two jobs and going to high school, shoot I was in like Flynn. Then when your mother found out that she and my mother went to Crispus Attucks together and in the same graduation class, she stopped referring to me as "that boy from down the street" and started calling me "Mr. Robert". I hope by the time we get married she'll just be calling me "Robert". Bob, do you remember all that? If you don't, I do. She could be somewhat intimidating at times. But being a single mother at that time with three teenage daughters I understood her being so let's say "cautious".

Well, since it's such a nice day and we have time for ourselves I'm going to run by the PX and then try and catch a movie at the four o'clock matinee. I love you so very much, Bob.

Love,
Robt.

Advanced Infantry Training

15 Oct 1969
Dear Bob Jr,

Bob, I got your pictures today and I love them. They'll help my loneliness for a while until I get some more.

In your last letter, you mentioned that you haven't been getting out. And, you asked the question "How did I feel about you going out with other boys?" Before I proceed with an answer I just want you to know I had to think long and hard, and this will be a tough letter for me to write. Bob, you know how I feel about you being alone and thus unhappy. For me that's a no no. When we were in high school those were the best days of our lives. The sports activities, social activities, the friends and the relationships we formed were not only fun but they also were essential for our growth and development. Bob, you worked hard for the opportunity to go to college. You graduated in the top 10% of our class of 360 at Attucks. You received many academic awards and honors, and several scholarships. Not only do you deserve it but you have earned this opportunity. And I want you to take full advantage of all that college has to offer, including the social life. I had my chance to go but I blew it. Studying was your first priority, playing sports and working two jobs were mine. Bob, I love you and I want you to take full

44

advantage of every good thing that life has for you. I understand what you're asking, and believe me "I KNOW" the risk that I face. But I'll take the risk now so you won't have any regrets later. This will be a test of our love for each other.

" *"A tough letter to write"*

Regarding your going out with other boys, I'm reluctantly OK with it. I'm OK with it because I trust you and I know you can handle yourself. When we were in high school you had many suitors, and you dealt with them in a very direct yet friendly manner. But in high school we were there together. At Ball State, I'm not there with you. But in my absence, I'm hoping the love that we have for each

other will give you the strength and wisdom of discerning who to go out with and how to conduct yourself while you're with them. Now for the reluctant part. Bob, you are a very intelligent, attractive, loveable and fun person to be with. With those qualities, someone is going to fall in love with you. They won't be able to help it. You may have some success controlling their actions but you won't be able to control their emotions or desires. That's why I'm somewhat reluctant. Now here's where I'm going to rely on my trust in you and my faith in God. Because if it's God's will for us to be man and wife than he will give you the strength to endure. I believe the Bible states that "He will not allow more than we can bear" (both of us).

Well, Bob, I'm going to end this letter. The subject was very deep. But sooner or later I knew we would have to discuss this issue. Plus, I'm not feeling well. I have a headache and my throat feels like it's on fire. I'm going to try and get a good night's sleep. By the way, how did you like your presents. And don't complain about the cost. I love you and my money loves you (smile).

Love,
Robt.

Advanced Infantry Training

18 Oct 1969
Dear Bob Jr,
I've got a confession to make. I've been a bad boy. The other day when we were on the Rifle Range during our break, I decided to be adventurous. Another soldier had some cigars and passed them out. I took one and smoked about a third of it. I lost about a third of my breakfast. Well, so much for me smoking cigars! Then a friend of mine had some chewing tobacco. He gave me just a little bit. Bob, I chewed it for about ten seconds before I spit it out. It was awful. Later on, that night we were in the barracks and the guy that bunks over me was smoking a pipe. I asked him if I could taste it. And Bob, it wasn't bad at all. If I were a smoker I

46

would probably smoke a pipe. So much for being adventurous!

"I love you a lottttttttttt"

Well, babe, about 39 more days to go then I'll be on my way home to you. Although it will be for just a little while, I'm going to enjoy every minute of it, especially the time I'm going to spend with you. I know that 39 days is a long time, but I found out if I keep my mind off it the time goes faster. My only problem is not keeping my mind off the 39 days. My problem is keeping my mind off you. Well, I've got to run. Their getting ready to show a movie in the day room and I want to get a good seat. I love you, Bob. And you know how much. A LOTTTT.

**Love,
Robt.**

Advanced Infantry Training
22 Oct 1969
Dear Bob Jr,
Bob, it's me again. I'm very tired today because they wore us out yesterday. We had a twelve-hour training day. Our subjects were Map & Compass Reading and Target Detection. Now I know Vietnam inside and out and I haven't even been there yet. The session was important because we learned the geography of the country and the different types of terrain that is characteristic of each geographical area. For example, the southern part of the country is flat and suitable for growing rice. It also has some very dense jungle areas. The very northern part of the

*country is a very mountainous region that is called the
Central Highlands. Those mountains are very dense with
vegetation and very steep. Right now, it's a very hot combat
zone. Along the Laotian and Cambodian borders, you have
a mixture of everything with very dense vegetation.
Compass reading was not easy, especially navigating
through the mountain regions. This training was very
important because in the event you get separated from your
main unit you have the capability to find them. Otherwise
you could be in very
serious trouble (lost).*

*Our last class of the
day was Target Detection.
In that class, we learned
how to detect non-moving
camouflaged targets in the
bush. That includes
detecting enemy soldiers,
bunkers and machine gun*

"The Bomb Picture"

*nests. Of all our training for some reason this session had
the most impact on the guys.*

*When we got back to the barracks the subject of
Target Detection came up in a very unusual and strange
way. Bob, now you have to keep in mind you're dealing
with a bunch of guys who are probably, no I would say who
are very horny, getting ready for bed. Carlos asked the
question, "Who could easily detect their woman in a crowd
or more specifically what is your woman's most
outstanding features?" I heard every answer from the size
of boobs, to the size of booties, how much makeup was
worn to long nails, wearing loud-colored clothes, I heard
everything. Although I kept silent through the whole thing I
was laughing like crazy. Then somebody called me out,*

"Hey, Wright, what do you have to say about your woman." I thought about my answer and then I said I would have to base my answer on let's say her character. "You see Bob is a"... Once I said Bob all hell broke loose. Some were asking, "Are you gay?" So, then I had to take them through the Bob & Bob scenario and they quieted down to hear my answer on the initial question, "What are the outstanding features of my woman?" So, this time I didn't waste any words I got right to the point. I told them that three of her attributes are tenderness, compassion, and expressing love. So, I see her outstanding features as her hands, her eyes, and her lips. When she wants to assure me of something, let's say her love for me she'll first take her hands and put them on the side of my face, she has very small soft hands. That's compassion. Second, she'll kiss me on my lips very softly yet firm enough that I can feel them, she has very soft lips. That's tenderness. And third, she will look me directly in my eyes and say, "Robert, I love you more than anything." That's expression. Then after about ten seconds of silence someone shouted out, "Well, all that sounds good, but what does she look like?" Bob, while he was saying that I went into my footlocker and pulled out the "bomb picture". Before I gave it to them I said, "And guys she just happens to have very beautiful legs." Then I went to the rest room while they passed your picture around. It was the one of you setting on the ground in front of your house modeling (for me) your gorgeous legs. When I returned everyone was in their bunks and I could see the picture lying on my bed. After I wiped the finger prints off the picture and put it back in my foot locker I went to the light switch flipped it off and said, "Lights out". Then out of the silence Carlos spoke out and said, "Well, at least we cleared up one thing, he's not gay."

Bob, I used our relationship as an example, to help them understand that the outstanding features of a loving relationship should be the expression of love between two people, and not the sole focus on body parts.

Bob, I have to stop writing now. It's time for chow. I'll try to call you next Friday. So, if you don't have a game or something try to be in your room between 8 & 10.

There is no place in my life for love unless I can share it with you.

Love,
Robt.

Advanced Infantry Training
01 Nov 1969
Dear Bob Jr,

How are you doing? Are you taking good care of yourself? Twenty-four more days until you'll be in my arms again.

Well, Bob, we have just returned from our five-day Bivouac. And let me tell you it was a very tough and challenging experience. The first three days wasn't bad. We participated in war games, went on all night ambush patrols and set up listening posts outside our camp areas. But on the fourth night it rained like crazy. Bob, we were soaked, muddy and cold. When we arrived back at our tents that night they were nice and dry on the inside but our clothes were soak and wet. And we had to sleep in those wet and muddy clothes all night. Our instructor who was very unsympathetic told us to quit crying and complaining. He said when we get to Nam it will be ten times worse. First, you won't be going on a five-day Bivouac. Depending on what unit you're assigned to, you could be out in the field on search and destroy missions from sixty to

50

ninety-days at a time. Second, you won't have tents you'll be sleeping on the ground under the stars every night. Third everything you need to survive you'll be carrying on your back, in a ruck sack that could weigh up to 60-70 pounds. And fourth, those wet clothes you were complaining about. Not only could they be wet from rain and mud but possible from your buddy's blood. And Bob, he said all that in a way that I don't think he was trying to scare us. He was telling it like it is. He's served two tours of combat duty in Vietnam.

The next day, which was Friday we had to pull down our tents and move out. For the rest of the day our training was focused on survival skills. The trucks arrived around four o'clock and we loaded up and headed back to the barracks. I was thinking about what the instructor said during the whole trip back.

Bob, over the last few weeks I've heard more and more about the realities of Vietnam. And it's a reality that I'm sure I'll have to face. Even as I sat in that truck with my head back and my eyes closed day dreaming I can see myself over there. The real scary part is when I ask myself do I want to go, part of me says no and part of me says yes. Why yes? You know Bob, maybe God has another level he wants to take me to,.especially before I take on the responsibilities of marriage and manhood. You know, when I look at my life today I have really been blessed. I have a good job at the Telephone Company awaiting me when I get out of the Service. I have a little money in the bank and most of all I have you. And believe me you're the best thing in my life. And I really don't deserve you. Maybe I need to experience life from a different perspective in order to appreciate why I've been blessed so. Well, let me tell you how we finished the day.

Bob, when we got back to the barracks we had to clean everything. Our weapons, bivouac stuff, our boots, the barracks and the latrine all before anyone could hit the sack. We were going to have barracks inspection at seven in the morning. There was mud everywhere. Well, we got it all done and passed inspection, but we stayed up all night.

Bob, thank you for your letters that I received this week. You'll never know what they mean to me. And that picture you sent setting in that chair was very nice. More, more, more!

Well, babe, I've got to go now so I can get some sleep. As a matter of fact, I'm sleep writing right now. In about two more weeks we have to spend a week on Peason Ridge. It's a replica of a Vietnamese Village.

Don't forget how much I love you. Keep the den warm so we'll have a nice warm place to say "I Love You" to each other.

Love,
Robt.

Advanced Infantry Training

02 Nov 1969

Dear Bob Jr.

How's it going? Is everything going well at school? I'm just a little moody today. I guess loneliness can eventually take its toll. Last night about 12:30 I took a chance and tried to call you but you weren't in. And today the phone booths were crowded all day. I spent most of the day to myself. You may ask how I can be so lonely with all those other soldiers around. Well, when I came to the realization that I will probably (99% sure) be sent to Vietnam, I have been listening to my instructors very closely. And when it comes to friendships in combat their advice is to follow this rule, "Be friendly but have very few friends." They say that not only will you have a good chance of surviving the war physically but also emotionally.

After Church, I took a nap around 1:00 P.M. The guys

"Being apart, is hard on the heart"

woke me up and asked me if I wanted to go with them to Leesville. I said "no" because I knew what they were going to Leesville for, prostitutes. They said, "Well, if you want to stay here and torture yourself that's your business." Bob, they don't understand what they consider as "torture" I consider it as "devotion". As a matter of fact, I haven't been off the base since the day we arrived. You see, babe, for me, "It's all about you, and only you".

Bob, as you can see I've had a lot of time to think about you today. I wish we could be together right now. Being apart is hard on the heart. That's a cute little saying that we say around here. But as for me it's a true saying. The next few days are going to go very slow.

Bob, I can't wait to get home and hold your hands. You know how much I love holding them. Their so soft and dainty, and very comforting. Our children will definitely know the difference between you holding them and me. And the left one is very special because it has my ring on it.

Bob, I won't be able to send you any pictures for a while because my camera is broken. I probably won't buy another one since I'll be home in a few days.

As for my birthday, other than you I don't know what I want or need. When you fell in love with me, that was my present for life. But, if you must get me something, give me something small and personal. Something that I can keep close and touch, that will remind me of you every day.

Hey, babe, I've got to go. It's 12 midnight and we're supposed to be up at 4:30 A.M. So, I'll end with "I love you".

Love,
Robt.

Advanced Infantry Training
06 Nov 1969
Dear Bob Jr,

How's life treating my sweetheart? I received a letter from mom today. The Telephone Company sent me another check for $326.33. Now I've got $652.66 in the *bank. Now I'll have some money to spend on you when I come home and still have a substantial balance.*

So, we'll have a nice time together. In addition, I'll get another  *check from the Telephone Company in about four weeks. That should bring my balance to over $800.00. That's not bad for two people who are not even married yet. Bob, I received another one of your pictures today. You are gorgeous. I love you so much. I'm really looking forward to our wedding day. For 103 pounds, you're perfect. Bob, you're so lovely I wanted to grab you right out of the picture. Well, I've got to run. I just wanted you to know that we won't be a poor couple. Especially as far as love is concerned!*

Love,
Robt.

Advanced Infantry Training

07 Nov 1969
Dear Bob Jr,

Do you still love me? So, what have you been up to these past few days? You haven't been getting evil, have you? Well, babe, it's down to nineteen days. Nineteen days until happy time. We'll be back in each other's arms again. We'll see if you still fit in my arms like you use to.

Bob, guess what, we get Veteran's Day off. But some of us might have to march in the Leesville Veteran's day Parade. I hope not. That means spit-shining boots and polishing brass. I'd rather just set in my bunk, pull out some of your pictures and just daydream about you.

Last night we were out until eleven o'clock training. We were conducting night patrols. It was a bad night for it because there was very little moon light so it was very dark. I mean it was almost pitch black. You couldn't see five meters in front of you. We were in a very wooded area and the trees had a lot of low-hanging branches. I got a few scratches on my face but they will heal by the time I get home. I made sure my shirt sleeves were rolled down so I wouldn't catch you know what, "poison ivy". I know, that's not funny.

Our patrol simulated a raid on a Viet Cong (VC) camp sight. And on the way back they hit us with an ambush to test our reaction time. I knew something was up when they had me on point and gave me an M-50 Winchester Shotgun. We used blank ammunition but it really felt like a real fire fight.

Bob, I got a letter from another girl yesterday. Her name was Mara A'Lynn Stuart. She wrote it on that three-line writing paper they use in grade school. It was a real

*surprise and I really appreciated it. Mara is like a little
sister to me.*

*Bob, when I get home you'll have to talk to me a lot.
We've been away from each other for close to four months
and after my leave I'll be gone again for a year. I want to
talk about you. I want to hear directly from you your
feelings and can you cope with all this. Am I asking too
much of you at this point in your life? I love you, Bob, and I
know you love me, but I want to be sure that we both
understand what we're committing ourselves to. Knowing
that you'll be there waiting for me will help me stay
focused and alert at all times. Alert to my day-to-day
situations and focused on my mission, to come back home
and marry you.*

*Well, I have to go. We're about to take off for another
day of patrolling. After that we're going to the range and
learn how to fire the 50-caliber machine gun. It fires a
bullet the size of my index finger. Looks like we'll be out
late again.*

Love,
Robt.

Advanced Infantry Training
10 Nov 1969
Dear Bob Jr,

*Guess where I've been for the past two days. In the
hospital. Friday afternoon we got two shots. And that night
after we had return from training it all started. When I
climbed into my bunk I began to get chills. Later on, in the
night I developed a terrible headache. But in the morning
when I tried to get up my back was so sore I could hardly
walk. So, they called an ambulance around 8:00 that*

57

morning to get me to the hospital. After the doctor examined me it was determined that I had a bad reaction to the shots given to us on Friday. They'll keep me in the hospital for observation the rest of the weekend. The Doctor said that I needed plenty of rest. So, I spent most of my time watching T.V. The food wasn't too bad. The nurses were young and cute but none of them were named Bob Jr. so I was just a patient. Today I convinced them I was doing much better, so they sent me back to my Company shortly after noon.

Bob, we finally got word we don't have to march in the Parade tomorrow. So, I'll be free on my birthday. If I can get together enough coins tonight I'll call you tomorrow.

Well, that's my weekend drama report. How did your weekend go? Fifteen more days and we'll see just how much we really missed each other. I can't wait to see the smile on your face.

I've got to stop here so I can try and round up some coins so I can call you tomorrow. So, remember I love you and I can't wait to see you again.

Love,
Robt.

Advanced Infantry Training
11 Nov 1969
Dear Bob Jr.

Happy Birthday to me! How does it feel to have a twenty-year-old future husband? I know that sounds kind of odd. But that's my mission. No, it won't be at age twenty but it won't be long. Bob your voice was so soft on the

58

phone last night I almost melted in my ventilated jungle boots.

Bob, I wished you had told me about this issue earlier. That's all I've been thinking about all day. Bob, again I want you to enjoy your College experience. You may have to be a little more direct and focused in regards to how you structure and manage your relationships. And remember what I told you, you can't control other people's feelings and emotions. But always remember I love you, I trust you and that we have a joint mission to fulfill in two years.

Bob, I have so much love in my heart to share with you; believe me, it will take a lifetime to fulfill. Although I'm only coming home on leave, I won't leave without ensuring you of my love for you, my devotion to you, and my commitment to your welfare and happiness.

Love,
Robt.

Advanced Infantry Training
12 Nov 1969
Dear Bob Jr,
How is my love waiting out the final days until my return? I received two more pictures today. You look great in that dress. That's the first time I've seen that one. I look forward to the day when I will see you in it in person. I sure miss you. Holding you in my arms again will be a sheer pleasure.

Bob, the love we have for each other is almost too good to be true. We've been together now for five years and have never broken up, or had any arguments and our love for each other is getting stronger. It's one of those "one

*chance in a million" scenarios. For the last two and a half
months all I've done was try to exist. But when I see and
hold you again I'll be alive again.*

    *Bob, our training has become more intense these
days. And it's more focused on combat tactics than
anything. We spend a lot of time in the field going through
maneuvers over and over and over. Don't get me wrong,
I'm not complaining. I'd rather do this than sit in a hot
class room all day. The more I' m in the field the more I'm
comfortable with being in the field. And don't worry, I
always have my eye out for poison ivy.*

    I've got to go. Love you; I'll be home in a few days.

Love,
Robt.

Advanced Infantry Training

17 Nov 1969
Dear Bob Jr,
    *How are you
today? Fine I hope. I'm
dead tired. Friday
morning me and eleven
other guys were
assigned to guard duty
on Tiger Ridge. We had
to stay up there all
weekend. We slept in*
*tents and ate C-Rations for the entire time. We returned to
the barracks this morning around 9 A.M. And guess what?
We have to go back to Tiger Ridge tomorrow with the
Company for training. We'll leave about 5 A.M. Advanced
Infantry Training is no joke. They're going to train us up to
the last minute. And I'm sure we're going to need it. Oh, I*

won't get my orders until next Monday. So, I'll know then if I'm going to Vietnam. I'm not going to worry about it until then. Whichever way it goes I'll be ready for it. I'll probably be more focused on being with you again rather than being the bearer of unpleasant news.

Bob, this will be my last letter from Fort Polk. Tomorrow you'll probably be sending your last letter, and I'll cherish it as much as I did the first.

Bob, you asked me in your last letter, "How I would feel about going to Vietnam?" Well, babe, to be honest personally I am a little scared. I don't care how well you're trained; going off to war for the first time at the age of twenty is very unsettling. But what's even more unsettling is worrying about you and Mom worrying about me. I won't be able to write nearly as much from Vietnam as I did in Basic Training or Advance Infantry Training. And if I know Mom, she'll be watching war coverage on the news channels every night. Every black soldier she sees (crawling, walking, running, or being carried) she'll think it's me. I hope Mr. D can keep her calmed down. Bob, in my spirit I know God will deliver me from this trial. I made a commitment to Him that I would be a good husband to you and I believe he'll give me a chance to fulfill that commitment. Now, your part, Mom's and the family's part are to Pray!

Bob, seeing you again will be like a dream come true. We have a lot of catching up to do. So, warm up your lips and do some pushups to strengthen your little arms, because we have a lot of kissing and hugging to catch up on. Ready or not here I come, you can't hide there's nowhere for "Bob Jr." to run.

Love,
Robt.

Army Processing Center - Seattle, Washington
17 Dec 1969
Dear Bob Jr,
    Bob, I am very sorry for the short amount of leave
time that we had. Fifteen days
was very short but we did try
to make the best of it. I'm glad
you did not have classes on
Friday. That gave us six full
days and two extra evenings
together. I hated to spoil
Christmas for everybody, but

Next Stop, "Vietnam"

Mom was very adamant about having it on the fifteenth
since I had to leave the next day. I just hated taking you
back to school that evening. That was hard for both of us.
I'm glad Michael rode with us. I had so much on my mind
(mostly you) it would have been hard for me to concentrate
on driving. Plus, on the way up he helped to keep the
conversation going. If it had been just the two of us we
probably would have been bawling the whole trip to
Muncie. I'm glad your roommate was there. It appeared to
me that she was there on purpose. Now that's a good
roommate. And I think she knew exactly what you would be
going through. This reminded me of the first time I took you
to Ball State. That was the first time we had been separated
since we started going together (3 yrs.). You cried for
almost three hours. It was almost 10 P.M. before I was able
to leave. But I didn't mind I would have stayed longer than
that if needed.
    Bob I'm going to miss you. Leaving you was very
hard. During the trip up Michael noticed that we were
trying to be strong for each other. This time we will be
separated for a year. We'll have to pray for each other

every day. God will touch us both spiritually and that will be the bond that holds us together. After this year is over, I'll have six and a half months left to do and that will be all downhill.

Oh, I almost forgot. Thank you for going with me to visit my grandmother before we left. She is crazy about you and I know, you think she's adorable. She gave me a little Bible with just the New Testament and Jesus' words are in red. She made me promise to read it and pray every day.

Now let me tell you where I'm at. I'm at the Army Processing Center in Seattle, Washington. Bob, this place is huge. For example, right now I'm in a room that has 600 bunk beds. Can you believe that? And, last night they were all occupied until this morning, when all but one was shipped (Airplane) out to Vietnam. I'm the only one still here. I'll probably go with the next bunch around 6 P.M. Bob, do you remember that syfi movie "Solvent Green" and how they processed humans in large groups. That's what it feels like here.

From here, I think we fly to Hawaii (we don't deplane), then to Guam and on to Vietnam. I'll try to write when I can. They're moving and processing us so fast. Hang in there, babe; I'll be in Nam in about another day and a half. When I get to my unit and get settled then I'll have time to reassure you that it's going to be all right. After I prayed this morning, I decided that I have to step up and show you I can be the man of our future family. No more crying or complaining. My focus is to make it back home and be with you the rest of my life. I know we were only able to spend a few days together but I think that was God's plan to keep me focused for the task that is before me. I love you, Bob!

Love, Robt.

63

Section 3: Combat Duty

South Vietnam - Central Highlands

Camp Evans Military Base *19 Dec 1969*
Dear Bob Jr.

Bob, we finally made it to Vietnam. I can't tell you where we landed, but I will say it was the busiest airbase that I've been on. The first thing we felt when we got off the plane was the heat. I'm sure we'll get used to it. It was about two hundred of us, all wearing brand new green jungle fatigues and green baseball caps. We looked like deer in headlights. Then we

101st AIRBORNE DIVISION

SCREAMING EAGLES

noticed about two-hundred other soldiers in old but clean fatigues waiting to get on the plane that we just got off. Their tours were over. They were going home. Once we were off and they started getting on. They started calling us "Cherries". There are a lot of things that soldiers say that have a sexual reference. Bob, soldiers that have not had any <u>physical</u> <u>contact</u> (actual combat) with the enemy are call "Cherries". You're a smart girl. I'll let you put 2 + 2 together.

Bob, the next thing we noticed was a refrigerated plane being loaded with black body bags, and they were not empty. That's something we probably didn't need to see. The guy standing next to me started freaking out. After I helped him get himself together, he looked at me and asked me, "Man, didn't that bother you?" I just looked at him and said, "Yes it did, but you better get used to dead bodies over here." Then he looked at me like I was strange or something. I probably should have told him that I worked part-time in a funeral home for the past five years.

Then on the opposite side of the Base we saw nothing but helicopters coming and going. One was loaded up with cases of Coke-a-Cola; another was loaded with cases of ammunition. Then we saw some soldiers (platoon size) wearing full combat gear loading into a Chinook Helicopter.

While we were still gazing around, all of a sudden, we were called to attention and marched to a big open field about one hundred yards away. There we were joined by about one thousand more soldiers. A staff sergeant got up on a small stage with a microphone and said, "At this time you will be assigned to your units and directed to the area designated for your unit. Now listen up people." He explained that he would call the name of the unit first, and then the names that he'd call after the unit name are those individuals who are assigned to that unit. Then you will police up (pick up) your gear and follow directions to where you are to assemble. So, Bob, I stood there for another 45 minutes then he called out, "The 101st Airborne Division." I knew that I wouldn't be assigned to that unit because I didn't go to jump school. I did not want to be a paratrooper. But after he read off about 40 names I heard my name called, "Wright, Robert E". I was stunned for a few seconds then I yelled out, "Sir, I did not go Airborne (jump school)." His response to me was (in a rough voice) "Son, you are now Airmobile, now grab your gear and move out." Bob, the next thing I knew we were on a Chinook Helicopter headed north to Camp Evans, home of the 2nd Battalion of the 506th Infantry Brigade (2/506) 101st Airborne Division. Bob, on the flight to Camp Evans being a part of the 101st was starting to grow on me. They're an elite fighting unit with a tough reputation that goes all the way back to World War II. I talked to some of the guys on the helicopter and they seemed to be OK with being assigned to this unit. And they all did well in Basic and Advance Infantry Training. Nobody talked stupid (heroic type). I can't wait to see what the rest of the Company is like. They're out in the field right now. I'll let you know later what they're like. I'm sure they're going to check me out too. After all I'm just a "Cherry" (smile). We waited in our make shift barracks for the Sergeant Major to come and give us our first briefing. They told us to take this time and write home, and let whoever is concerned about you know that you have made it this far.

I love you, Bob, I love you very much, and I'll always stay focused on our mission (marriage). You do the same.

FOCUS! FOCUS! FOCUS! I'll try and write you again tonight.

Love,
Robt.

"This is my command be strong and courageous! Do not be afraid or discouraged. For the Lord your God is with you wherever you go."
Joshua 1:9 NLT

Camp Evans Military Base
21 Dec 1969
Dear Bob Jr,
Over here it's Sunday morning and I just got back from Church. Boy, I sure miss Black Preaching. Don't get me wrong, the Inter-Denominational Ministers are great. But every once in a while, you know what I mean. However, there is one thing that the Military Church has in its favor; everybody has on the  *same outfit. I try to read the little Bible that my grandmother gave me every day. And I really enjoy it.*

I'm sorry I didn't get to write you a second letter Friday but we were very busy the rest of the day. We had to get the rest of our gear including our M-16 Rifles. And as soon as you get your weapon the first thing you do is clean it. Especially if it's used. Then on Saturday we went to the range and fired every weapon we learned to shoot in Advance Infantry Training. They trained me on a new weapon, the 90-Millimeter Recoilless Rifle. I'll tell you about that one later. The Company is out in the field and they won't be back until sometime before New Year's Eve. So, the Sergeant Major is going to hold me back, and I'll go out with the Company after New Year's. But in the mean time he's got another team he wants me to train and work with starting tomorrow. So, we'll see what he has in store for me. Now I won't have to go on bunker guard tonight. It's movie night at Church tonight. They're showing "The Ten Commandments". You know I don't want to miss that.

Bob, I won't be able to write as much as I did at Fort Knox and Fort Polk. I found out in our briefing Friday that when we go out to the field we're on 90-day search and destroy missions. And we're limited to how much we can carry. That includes writing materials. I'll write at least once a week. But I need to hear from you as much as possible. I need to know you're there and focused on our future. I know I will be. We're trained to focus on God and Country. My focus is on God, Country, and Bob Jr. Stay sweet and be strong.

Love,
Robt.

Oh, FYI, for fear that they could fall into enemy hands we are not allowed to keep letters from home. Especially when we're on combat missions. If they fall into enemy hands they will send false information home. Or if we're taken as prisoners they will send pictures home of us

68

being tortured. Your letters will be well-read before I destroy them.

Camp Evans Military Base

22 Dec 1969
Dear Bob Jr.
Good morning (or evening) how is my sweetheart doing today? I'm doing great. I just keep thinking about you and staying "focused on the future". I met with the Sergeant Major (Top) about this team he's putting me on (no, I don't have any choice). It's a LZ cutting team. An LZ cutting team cuts the trees and clears vegetation off the tops of hills that maybe suitable sites for Helicopter Landing Zones. LZ's are used for future troop deployment or extraction. Each Company in the Battalion is to send one man to be on the team. The designated hill top should be in an area where there has been no enemy activity for at

Old Landing Zone (LZ)

"Rappelling"

least 45 days. The team uses explosives, shovels, power saws, and axes to do the job. Now here's the hairy part. The team has only seven men, they make a lot of noise and most of the time they have to repel (lower themselves to the ground on nylon ropes from 80 feet up) on or around the base of the hill. The goal is to cut the LZ that day and be picked up before dusk. The Choppers will land on the finished LZ, we'll load up with our equipment and get out of there. What you don't want to happen is to have to stay out overnight. With a seven-man team and limited ammo, you don't want to engage the enemy in a prolonged firefight. Now you're going to ask me, "Isn't that dangerous?" And my answer is "yes". You're making so much noise that anyone for miles around will know where you are. But I have resigned myself to the fact that everything we do is going to be dangerous. That way I won't let my guard down at any time. Remember, babe, to get through this year we have to "Stay Focused on Our Future!!" True-love will endure the past, present, and future.

Love,
Robt.

Camp Evans Military Base
    25 Dec 1969
    Dear Bob Jr,
    Merry Christmas! I know it's not the same but I'm not going to complain. Although we can't celebrate it together the reason for the season has not changed. I know one thing though; I miss you very much

"Merry Christmas"

especially today. You know Christmas is my holiday. I hope you got a chance to get down to my mom's. I know she would love to see you. Seeing you would cheer her up.

Unfortunately, things are going to be very hectic around here today. Yesterday evening the whole Battalion came in from the field for "stand down". They'll probably be in through the Holidays. Yesterday things didn't go to well. Alfa Company and Charlie Company were attacked. Between the two they had seven casualties, six wounded and one KIA. This will be a sad Christmas season for their families. One guy told me to "Get used to it, we're not in a John Wayne movie it's a real war and we're in it." Later on, that day I found out the person who gave me that advice was my Platoon Leader. I'm in Alfa Company, 2nd Platoon, 2nd Squad.

For the rest of the day I'm going to take advantage of every meal the Mess Hall serves today. I'll try to talk to some of the guys in my Squad, if they'll talk to me. Remember I'm still a Cherry. I'll spend some time in my bunk area reading my Bible and thinking about you and all those Christmases we've spent together. You know Bob, if you really stop and think about it, we were inseparable. I remember the time we came back from a movie and your mother asked us, "Barbara Anne, Robert, don't you ever get tired of each other." You said "No" and I said "No ma'am." Later on, this evening they'll be showing a movie about the Nativity at Church. I don't want to miss that.

I'm glad you won't get this letter before Christmas. The Sergeant Major informed me to be on the Helicopter Pad Tuesday the 28th at 0:500 (5 A.M.) in full combat gear. The LZ team is going out to cut our first LZ.

I love you, Babe, and I hope you enjoy your Christmas. And "Stay Focused on our Future!!!"

**Love,
Robt.**

71

Camp Evans Military Base

27 Dec 1969
Dear Bob Jr,

Bob, I had to get up early this morning to attend a crash course (6 hours) on demolition in preparation for our mission tomorrow. Our LZ cutting team is going out for the first time. The training was basically on the overall work, methods and responsibilities of cutting and clearing LZ's. We learned when to use explosives and when not to use explosives. We also learned the way to use and maintain our more conventional equipment, like chain saws and axes. We were also instructed on the proper way to clear an LZ. You to start from the outward edges and work your way to the center. This will keep debris out of your way and help to establish defensive cover while you're working. And, how to use the large tree trunks to build night defensive areas in the event you had to stay overnight. Then we went over safety items. The main areas on safety were: (1) keep two men on guard at all times. even when you're staying overnight, (2) keep your helmet on at all times, (3) before setting off explosives you must yell "Fire in the Hole", (4) when downing tress with conventional equipment (regardless of the size of its diameter) you must yell "Timber", (5) make sure you leave nothing behind that the enemy could use. Bob, that's a lot to learn in six hours. Now I see why Veterans are a valuable resource. They are multi-talented, they know how to take risks, and they can take on a lot of responsibility. Oh, and don't let me leave this out, "They know how to work as a team."

Bob, if you could ask me a question right now you would probably ask whether I was scared or nervous." Well, I'm a little of both. I'm a little nervous now because I've been thinking about this all day. I'll probably be scared tomorrow because we are very likely to have enemy contact.

"Ready, Willing & Waiting"

But there's another emotion that I'm experiencing and that is my adrenalin is pumping. Maybe these are the emotional phases you go through before you go into action. If so, I'll know after tomorrow. And yes, with all these emotions having an effect on my actions I won't forget to "Stay Focused on Our Future". And Bob, for me that means I have to "Stay Alert, do my Job and Stay Alive!" My end game or mission is to come home, marry you, have kids, and live happily ever after. Love you very much!!

Love,
Robt.

Camp Evans Military Base
29 Dec 1969
Dear Bob Jr.

Bob, our mission yesterday was a success. This was my first official combat mission in Vietnam. We arrived at our destination around 0:700 (7 A.M.). However, we did have to repel (80 ft. ropes) out of the Helicopter. And guess who was selected to go first. Being first on the ground is kind of scary. If the Choppers receive heavy ground fire and have to pull out then I'm stuck on the ground by

73

*myself. That didn't happen so I made out OK. I was down
and off the rope in five seconds. I moved out about 15
meters and took up a defensive position and waited for the
rest of the team to descend and gather all our equipment. I
see why our training at Fort Polk was so repetitive. My
actions were more instinctive rather than reactionary (what
do I do now, what do I do next). We got our equipment up
the hill and took a short break (steep hill). We posted two
perimeter guards and got to work. Between explosives*

*going off and chain saws
running we made a lot of
noise. But everything went
smoothly. After we finished
cutting the LZ we gather all
our equipment together at the
top of the hill. And around
1400 hours we called on the
radio and asked for immediate
pick up. When the Helicopters*

"1st Mission to the Field"

*where in route we started taking small arms fire from our
rear. The shots were coming from lower ground about 75
meters out. There were possibly two, no more than three
shooters. So, we returned fire with our M-16's. Once we
got their heads down we saturated the area with grenade
fire from our M-79. That seemed to do the trick. We did not
receive any more gun fire from that area. Our team leader
said that they were either dead or running like hell. Then
we heard the Helicopters coming up the valley. They
landed on the newly cut LZ, we loaded up our equipment
and we were headed back to Camp Evans. Mission
accomplished.*

*Bob, you know what this means. I'm not a "Cherry"
any more. In that contact with the enemy I emptied three*

74

magazines from my M-16 (a total of 45 bullets) and threw
one grenade. And, I heard the authentic cracking sound of
an AK-47. Through that whole ordeal was I nervous? Was I
scared? Yes. But I was also "Focused on Our Future". I've
got to go to debriefing. I'm okay, but I'll say this, "Combat
is no joke."

Love,
Robt.

Camp Evans Military Base
01 Jan 1970
Dear Bob Jr.
Happy New Year!
    I'm starting this letter at 12:01 A.M. New Year's
Day. This is as close as I can get, babe. I took a long nap
yesterday and when I woke up I just laid in my bunk and
thought about you. I figured you probably went to a dance
New Year's Eve night having fun. And for some reason I
started thinking about our High School Junior Prom. I
think that was the first dance you got me to go to. Although,
I did ask you. We were so proud to be with each other that
night. You were so pretty and petite and I was so serious
and debonair. That whole week I was so excited about
taking you to the dance of the year. I did everything I could
to create a fairytale night for you. I wanted that night to be
a night you'd never forget. A night so magical that after it
was over it would remain in our hearts forever. I remember
when we got to the Prom we spent so much time just
walking around holding hands we only danced twice. But
we didn't care we were more interested in others seeing us
together. Later on, that night after we kissed each other
goodnight at that moment we both understood how deeply

we loved one another. That night we secretly committed ourselves to get married some day and since then we are still committed to being together for the rest of our lives. What a magical night that was.

"High School Junior Prom"

I also believe that was the night our identities changed. We went from being Barbara Hampton and Robert Wright to Bob Jr. & Bob Sr. And, by the end of our Senior Year I believe we were the model couple of the class of "68". We had been together the longest and everyone knew our relationship was based on

"Pretty and petite, serious and debonair"

true love rather than popularity.

*I'll close with I miss you, I love you, and let's stay focused on the commitment we made to each other on prom night. **"Oh, What A Night."***

Love,
Robt.

02 Jan – 14 Jan 70
No Letters Found for This Period

Camp Evans Military Base
15 Jan 1970
Dear Bob Jr,

How are you today? I'm doing fine. We're still at base camp (Evans). I'm hearing we may be here through the TET Cease Fire. And that's fine with me. There's a lot of enemy activity and movement in the I Corps (Central Highlands) region and they want to refortify and strengthen the Defensive Perimeter (bunker line) that surrounds Camp Evans. Oh, by the way do you remember that first LZ we cut a few days ago? Well, a Recon Team used it for their mission and found two dead North Vietnamese Army regulars in the area where we returned fire. Now we know all that noise does draw attention. Especially if there aren't any other friendly ground forces operating in the area.

That means when we go back out again to cut an LZ we're going to have to be a little more creative setting our defensive perimeter.

Bob, regarding the issue of our getting married when I get home at the end of the year. You know that marrying you is my main mission in life. But when we get married I want to start that phase of our lives together with you. Not separated again. And

Bob & Bob

that's not possible this year. When I finish my tour in Vietnam and take some leave time I'll still have six and a half months before I complete two years of active duty. Until then I won't know where I'll be stationed. I'm pretty sure it will be state-side but I won't know where until then. But I will be within phone distance. Bob, when we get married I don't want it to be a ceremony, hang out for a few days, and then grab my bags and fly off somewhere. I'm not Superman and you're not Lois Lane. We're Bob & Bob. We are one in the same.

Bob, getting married is a permanent move. After the ceremony, I want to take you home and be with you for the rest of our lives, rather than suffer through another painful separation. But I will tell you this, when you plan for graduation also plan for our wedding.

I know what's going on; you're probably getting pressured by someone. Just stay "focused," study hard, and most of all, remember how much we love each other. We'll get through this, I promise!

Love,
Robt.

Camp Evans Military Base
19 Jan 1970
Dear Bob Jr,

How are things going for you? Anything new since my last letter? I'm doing OK. I've got a lot to tell you but let me start off with "I love you, I miss you, and I'd give anything to be with you right now." Most people will never know or understand what it's like to be separated from someone you love because of war or conflict. At times I feel so lonely and helpless. Memories and day dreaming help, but nothing can replace the power of your touch or the magic in your voice. Nothing!

Well, Bob, early Saturday morning we went out to cut our 2nd LZ. This one didn't go as smooth as the first one. The first mishap came when we had to repel again and guess what? I got hung up in a tree (don't laugh). The next problem was the foliage was so thick and the hill was so steep, it took us most of the day to get our equipment up the hill. As a result, we had to stay out overnight and start the next morning. We found a nice thicket to set up in for the night, and booby trapped a couple of claymore mines and set out trip flares to extend our perimeter. It rained most of the night and we were cold and miserable all night. About 2 A.M. we heard some movement but it was far enough away we did not engage it. The next morning, cold and wet, we got up early and started cutting the LZ. We left our claymores and flares out for additional protection and early warning. We finished the LZ around 3 P.M. and radioed for pick up. We were told that all the Helicopters were working down south and would not be available for a couple of hours. So we waited.

Well, around 5 P.M. it started raining hard. And before long we realized we were socked in (heavy cloud cover over the mountains). When the Helicopters came they couldn't find us. They couldn't see our colored smoke. We could hear them but we couldn't see them. So they had to abandon the mission and we had to stay out another night. Bob, we all looked at one another and felt totally abandoned. But we learned later on that two nights in the field was a picnic. When the Battalion goes back out in the field our missions will be 60-90 days. Our problem now was just getting through tonight. We had plenty of food and ammo, our worry was what Charlie (North Vietnamese Regulars) was going to be up to tonight. Then it started raining again. Bob, it rained so hard we started sliding down the hill (I told you the mountains were steep). To deal with that problem we dug six-inch-deep, six-foot-long trenches to lie in. We virtually laid in mud all night. And you could count on one hand how many hours of sleep we got. We rotated guard shifts three on and three off for ten hours. If Charlie had come that night, he would have to fight a steep wet mountain, all the wood and debris from cutting the LZ, claymore mines, and seven very nervous but alert GI's. We spent the next day waiting to be picked up. Around 4 P.M. the Helicopters arrived with a Cobra Gunship escort. We blew the claymore mines for cover and loaded up and headed back. God was surely with us. On the trip back to Camp Evans, I thought about the story we read in Sunday School about the three Hebrew Boys in the burning fiery furnace. Bob, Jesus was walking all around that mountain. We were cold, wet, muddy, tired, and eventually saved.

Bob, you and Mom must be doing a lot of praying. We spent three days and two nights on that LZ and did not come in contact with the enemy. Now that was a blessing. And its three days closer to you.

Love,
Robt.

Camp Evans Military Base
24 Jan 1970
Dear Bob Jr,
I wonder what you're doing know. More than likely you're still asleep. But that's okay. The more sleep you get the more beautiful you'll be when I get home.
Yesterday we cut another LZ. You know it would be nice if we could use a little cement, then my initials (REW)

would be all over Vietnam. This one wasn't too bad however I did get a little banged up. This guy was cutting down a small three and when it fell he forgot to yell "timber". I didn't hear it fall because I was running a chain saw. The small tree hit me across the back of my neck. I was dizzy for a couple of hours, but recovered after I got over the dizziness. And it didn't bleed too much (sorry no purple heart). After we finished the LZ, by the request of the Battalion Commander we had to stay overnight. He wanted us to set up an ambush. He wanted to see if the NVA (North Vietnamese Army) would come around the LZ looking for anything we might have left behind. Bob, that's when I realized that to some we were expendable. So, we stayed overnight but the enemy did not show up. They picked us up about 10 A. M. this morning.

Bob, I'm sorry to say that the PX at Camp Evans doesn't have any cameras. Because they probably prefer that we not take pictures in the field. I need you to send me a small camera like the one you sent me at Fort Polk.

Well, Bob, how have you been doing? Do you still love me? I know you do but I just like to read your "yes". I love you, in fact I love you so much that I think about you not just some of the time but "ALL" the time. You wouldn't believe the time I spend thinking about you. As a matter of fact, if I were to write you every time I thought about you, it would take all the writing material available at the PX. Also, if the Army knew how much I think about you they would Court Marshall me for dereliction of duty. And that doesn't include my dreams. Bob, I know it's a little early to be talking about coming home, but sense I think about it I may as well talk about it (it makes sense to me).

Bob, I know when I get home, if you're home from school you'll want to come to the airport and pick me up.

But at times I think about different ways of surprising you. I may even rent a car at the airport and surprise you and Mom. Don't worry, I still know my way to Ball State. It will be interesting to see how we interact with each other. I've talked to some of the guys who are here on their second tours. They say coming home from combat duty in Vietnam is a lot different than coming home from Basic Training or AIT. They say you'll be rediscovering everything. From turning on a light switch, enjoying endless hot showers, and more importantly relating to personal relationships. You'll be very unsure of your actions. As a result, you tend to be shy at times. And breaking Military habits will take time. So, that means you'll have to initiate the kisses and "affirmative" means that "I agree".

Well, Bob, I've got to go I need to get some sleep. You know by now it's impossible to get any sound sleep in the field, especially on ambush. Nobody is supposed to be sleep on ambush. Oh, if you can get anymore spare time please write. I love you and stay "Focused on the Future".

Love,
Robt.

Firebase Jack
27 Jan 1970
Dear Bob Jr,
Bob, how are you? Are you okay? Is there something wrong? The reason I'm asking these concerning questions is I haven't heard from you in three weeks. So far, this month I've received two letters from you the first week, ten from Mom, and she has mentioned you in some of hers. Also, I've received two from Mike, two from Mr. D, and one from Joyce. If I don't hear from you soon I will be very

*worried. Everybody is teasing me because every time I get
a letter it's from my mom. I don't care about the teasing.
I'm concerned about you. Being this far from you I feel so
helpless. Please write me and let me know that you're okay.*

*In my last letter, I mentioned we were going to
Firebase Jack. It's a fire base designed to Support Camp
Evans in case there
is a mass attack from
the Central
Highlands. It's
located about one
and a half miles
south of Camp
Evans. It's designed
to deliver massive
fire power
(casualties) to stop*

Approaching Firebase Jack

*any massive enemy attack from the south. Things are
starting to heat up. Camp Evans was hit last night with
Mortars and Small Arms fire. This morning a Helicopter
was shot at and the door gunner was hit in the leg. Last
night we even heard movement outside our perimeter.*

*Bob, last night I was thinking about you. I was
wondering what you looked like at that very moment. What
were you wearing, what were you doing, yes and whether
or not you were smiling? But most of all I thought about
our wedding day, because I know you'll be smiling that
day. We'll be a very happy couple. Life will be good for us.
And we'll be good for each other. I'll work hard. Since I
couldn't make you proud when I was playing basketball in
High School, maybe I can do better as a Telephone Man. At
least I won't be sitting on the bench. I still think I can make
it in college, but there will be time for that later. After I*

finish my service obligation my focus will be on us and our future. Bob, I was very proud of you when I saw your picture at the State Fair as a Ball State University Cheerleader. Then I looked back at my life and asked, "What have I done on that level to make you proud of me?"

I know you'll say it doesn't matter, because you're in love with me. But I care. I want to be someone you can be proud of the way I'm proud of you.

Well, babe, until my next letter remember how much I love you. And may your love for me keep growing as much as my love is growing for you.

Love,
Robt.

Firebase Jack
03 Feb 1970
Dear Bob Jr,

Bob, I got your letter today and in regards to what you're going through. Again, I'm not surprised. I knew that this stage of my military service would be the hardest for both of us. I knew that sooner or later you would get terribly lonely, especially in the mist of the glamour and romance of College life. I know that on one hand you want to be a part of it but on the other hand it may conflict with being a part of me. And it's hard to juggle both, especially when the lives (feelings, emotions, hopes and desires) of others are involved. On one hand, there's an environment

84

of parties, togetherness, romance, and day to day relationships. On the other hand, there are only letters and memories. In an effort to juggle these things you're struggling with the day-to-day decision of how high up do I throw this ball and how low do I let the other ball fall before I catch it. Or which ball will I eventually let fall to the ground.

Bob, the answer you seek won't come from what's going on around you or who's speaking to you. Those are temporary, impromptu influences that most often have a negative effect on long term decisions. You're going to have to resolve this internally and not from outside pressure. In other words, you have to follow your heart. Let your "heart" guide you rather than what you hear and see around you. Don't let your current circumstance cloud the future that God has planned for you.

Bob, when I end my letters with stay "Focused on the Future" that's not just a jingle that I dreamed up. It's a reflection on our past in regard to what we have planned for our future. I don't see Bob & Bob as just a tag from high school, I see it as a brand burned in our hearts that we can touch and feel forever. So, Bob, what you see around you may not be what God has planned for you. I love you so much. You have been a very important part of my life for the past four and a half years. My life would be so empty without you. The day we see each other again will be a wonderful day, life will begin all over again. I'm going to make you very happy, Bob. And time will tell.

Love,
Robt.

Firebase Jack
06 Feb 1970
Dear Bob Jr,

Bob, how are things? Do you feel any better than you felt from your last letter? I hope so. I hope my last letter helped.

Well, Bob last night was the second night of TET. I'm sure you've heard about the TET Offensive on the news. Nothing happened last night. But tonight, when I go on guard I'll be extra careful. We found out that on the fourteenth of the month our Company may be moving down south. I hope not. They have too many booby traps. And you know by now I'm a mountain man (smile).

Bob, I can't write too long because we have to get as much sleep as possible during the day. So, we can be wide awake at night. But I wanted to get an "I love you" in regardless. I'm so fortunate to have you home waiting for me. Maybe I'll get lucky and dream about you. If I do we'll probably have an Air-Raid and the sirens will wake me up just when I'm in the middle of a kiss. "Focus on the Future."

> ***Love,***
> ***Robt.***

Firebase Jack
07 Feb 1970
Dear Bob Jr,

You're probably sound asleep now. It's twelve noon over here. It rained early this morning but it has stopped now. Last night was the third night of TET and I'm happy to say things were pretty quiet.

Bob, the days and nights go so fast over here. I hope time isn't going too slow for you back home. What are they saying about the War at home? What is President Nixon doing besides visiting? I heard on the radio that he's planning on visiting Indianapolis and Chicago.

Would you believe I'm having an issue with some of the "Brothers"? They're upset because I won't smoke (marijuana) with them. I told them I don't want it, I don't need it, and it's illegal. I don't want it because I want my head to be clear at all times. I don't need it because I stay "Focused", and Bob, you know what on. And because it's illegal I don't want to get caught with it and have to spend time in the stockade. I don't want to spend any more time in this country than I have too.

Bob, what are the top records back home. Over here we listen to Soul Train on the radio from 8 – 10 P.M. The top five tunes are: (1) Want You Back – J5 (2) Psychedelic Shack – Temptations (3) Going in Circles – Friends of Distinction (4) Message from a Black Man – Temptations (5) Some Day We'll Be Together – Supremes.

Well, I've got to go. I'm going to try and write Mom before I take a nap. Try to smile and remember, "I love you very much."

Love,
Robt.

Firebase Jack
08 Feb 1970

Dear Bob Jr,

First, I want to know did you go to church today? I went this morning after my guard shift. Yes, I took a shower first. Second how are you feeling, is your school work getting any better?

Well, Bob, last night was the fourth night of TET. Tonight, will be the last. Tomorrow morning the TET cease fire will be over.

How are situations back home? Have you been home lately? What are Lisa and David doing?

Bob, last night I was thinking about the guy you've been going out with. On one hand, I envy him because he has the pleasure of being near you. And here I am thousands of miles away fighting in a war. However, on the other hand, your love is reserved for me. But Bob, when I get home, I'll be the envy of everyone because your date book will be filled up for the rest of your life. Of course, the name on it will be changed from Barbara A. Hampton to Mrs. Robert E. Wright. And your husband (me of course) will fill all the pages. You know, Bob, I thank God for giving me so much (love, joy, happiness and hope) in one small package, "you." You're something very special to me. You're the one that I will always love. You're my past, present, and future.

Well, babe, I've got to go now. I have to get some ammo for my M-16. Tell everybody that you , ME!!!

Love,
Robt.

Firebase Jack
09 Feb 1970

Dear Bob Jr,

I know I've said this over a thousand times but if you don't mind I'll say it again, "I love you." I have been blessed with a very lovely and passionate young lady, whom I love and cherish with all my heart. Bob, I live each and every day for you. You mean that much to me. I'm still amazed at how fast I fell in love

"Bob, how did you do it?"

with you. How did you win my love so quickly and so completely? I would like to know. And don't tell me it was those so-called powers you claim to have. Well, however, you did it, the fact is you did it. And I have no complaints what so ever.

Well, Bob, this is a short letter so I tried to make it sweet and sincere. Until tomorrow, love always.

Love,
Robt.

Firebase Jack
10 Feb 1970
Dear Bob Jr.

Hi, babe. I hope you're feeling good today because I am. Today I got some letters from Mom. And I got one from the guys at the garage. Bob, I wish you could read it. It's very nice. I'm also happy because when I get a letter from Mom I get one from you the next day. How do you like the picture I sent? That's me (of course) holding a 90-millimeter recoilless rifle. I only use it at the fire base. If the firebase is attacked my assistant gunner (he loads the 90-millimeter rounds) and I am responsible for destroying as many of the enemy ground troops as possible. The sand boxes behind me are used to block the back blast. We spent most of the morning practicing on hitting targets and reloading fast enough to stop a mass attack.

Bob, I've got to go now. We have just picked up on radar troop movement about two thousand meters out

headed our way. And we don't have any friendlies in that direction. I've got to go and get this "90" set up. Don't worry I'll be careful. Besides, I'll still have my M-16 beside me.

I'll mail this letter tomorrow so you'll know I'm okay.

Love,
Robt.

Firebase Jack

13 Feb 1970
Dear Bob Jr,

It's about 2:30 A.M. and I just came off guard. By the way that movement that we picked up on Radar was NVA Troops. But instead of them coming here Radar traced them changing directions and heading back up in the mountains. They probably found out that "Wildman" Wright was on the 90-Millimeter (laugh).

So far tonight it has been pretty quiet. I've got to go back on guard at 5:40 A.M. Bob, tonight I found out that we're not going south until September. That's good news. The one thing I've learned over here is the longer it takes for them to make up their minds about something the least likely it will happen. But, I also found out that since TET is over we'll be going out in the field. Not to cut LZ's, but at company strength (150 men). Our primary mission will be "search and destroy". "Bob, it's prayer time."

Bob, regarding your friend I've come to the conclusion that the dating scenario is not working for both of you. He's trying to grow the relationship and you're trying to keep it stabilized. And it's not really working for either of you. He's romantically frustrated and you're emotionally challenged. In regards to me, I sense you're experiencing some feelings of betrayal and in regards to him, you're feeling guilty because your commitment to a relationship is limited. You're both going in opposite directions. Bob, as we say in the Army, "You're going to have to take command" and let him know that going forward any relationship between the two of you has to be on friendship basis only. Hopefully that will limit his expectations and settle your day to day anxiety and help you to pay more attention to your studies. If that doesn't work, there's an old saying, "Sometimes to preserve what you got, you have to tighten the lid on the jar to keep the contaminants out."

Well, Bob, I've got to get a couple of hours of sleep before I go back on guard. Bob, I love you and I miss you very much. My heart cries out for you every day. Always remember to stay "Focused on our Future".

Love,
Robt.

14 Feb – 23 Feb 70
No Letters Found for This Period

Field Mission (Search and Destroy))
24 Feb 1970
Dear Bob Jr,
Bob, yesterday was not a good day for us. Yesterday morning we were hit and hit bad. We were on an LZ waiting for our resupplies when all of a sudden, all hell broke loose. We got hit with RPG's (NVA rocket propelled grenades), machine gun fire, and small arms fire. We were able to return fire but not quick enough before they took off. It was like an ambush. We had eight casualties. Some were wounded, some were KIA. I lost my Squad Leader and a guy I met from Detroit. Right away our Platoon Leader repositioned us to extend our perimeter, while others helped with the wounded. Those of us who were on guard were about thirty meters from the main group and twenty meters apart from each other. Bob, it seemed like I was out there all by myself. I was scared but I was alert. Then we got word that the Medevac Choppers would be coming in and to stay alert. I checked my weapon to make sure I had a round in the chamber and it was off safety. I put an extra magazine in my helmet band pulled out a grenade and I was in a squat position with my eyes and ears focused on the jungle in front of me.
Behind me I could hear a lot of commotion and the RTO (Radio Operator) talking to the pilot of the inbound Chopper. Believe it or not all that commotion kind of

92

settled me down. It also gave me a sense of purpose. Bob, at that moment I felt that it was my job to make sure that if we were counter attacked they would not get through my position. I didn't feel like a hero, but I did understand my responsibility to my Platoon to defend my position.

Bob, you know how much I watched War Movies on TV and at the drive-in. Well, now I know the difference between entertainment and the real thing. Bob, my focus

Medevac Helicopter

for the next ten months is being alert and being ready. After the Medevac Helicopters arrived and picked up our casualties, we got ready to move out to an emergency LZ to receive our resupply.

Bob I've got to end now. I've got first shift on guard tonight and everybody's still pretty touchy from yesterday. I love you, don't forget to pray.

Love,
Robt.

Field Mission (Search and Destroy)
28 Feb 1970
Dear Bob Jr.

Bob, how are you doing today? I'm doing okay considering that we walked into a booby trap today. It happened early this morning. I and four other GI's went out on a patrol ahead of the platoon. We were headed down a steep hill with full ruck sacks, so it was pretty hard going. If it wasn't for the small trees to grab hold of we probably would have slid down the hill. And I think Charlie (Viet Cong) knew that. Well, one of our Squad Leaders was leading the patrol when he slipped, grabbed a small tree, and then started rolling downhill. About two seconds later we heard a metallic click followed by a very loud explosion. We had set off a booby trap. In no time four other guys including our medic showed up to assess the situation and give us a hand. The Squad Leader was okay; he had fallen away from the blast. I was okay except for the ringing in my ears. That's probably because I was bringing up the rear of the patrol. The three guys in the middle were caught in the middle of the blast. That's what we call the kill zone. Two had very serious wounds to the chest and one had a serious leg wound. We made stretchers out of our ponchos and got them to an LZ ASAP. After the wounded were extracted we were on the move again but in a different direction. Later on, we found out all three men were going to be okay. Plus, they all had million-dollar wounds (that means they're going home).

Bob, later on I talked to the Squad Leader who led our patrol, and he said if it wasn't for our spacing (distance between one another) we probably would have all been very seriously wounded. He asked me where I took my Advanced Infantry Training. I told him at Fort Polk. He said he had heard that's one of the best. That was good to hear. And to think when I first got there I was always complaining. Now I find out that I was well-prepared. Even for the heat and the bugs.

Well, like I said in one of my last letters, "This is no John Wayne movie." Bob, just so you'll know I'm not going to tell you everything that happens. Just enough to give you some idea of what it's like over here without worrying you too much. I know you are going to worry some, but let me do the bulk of the worrying. You just keep praying and telling me that you love me.

Love,
Robt.

Field Mission (Search and Destroy)
02 Mar 1970
Dear Bob Jr,

I think today is Monday, I don't know. When you're out in the field, believe me, all the days just seem to run together. We had an extremely hard day today humping through the bush. In this mountainous region, the only way to get from point A to point B is to go over the mountains. I mean steep mountains. Long mountain ranges. But, at all cost we have to keep moving. We're safer if we keep moving.

And staying on the move is not our worst problem. It's hygiene. We haven't had a bath in daysssssssss. In the field, there's only

"We need a bath, bad."

three ways of getting one: (1) a waterfall, (2) when it rains, and (3) a stream or pond. Streams and ponds, you have to be careful because of leaches. Blood sucking leaches. If they get into the wrong openings, well, let's just say you're in deep trouble.

And Bob, you haven't seen nothing yet until you see these bugs. Vietnam has every bug over here that we have at home. The only difference is they're three times as big. At night when you're on guard and your face is uncovered, the mosquitoes sound like World War II suicide fighter planes. And the red ants are so bad they leave red bite marks all over your neck. The mosquito/bug repellent is so thick and potent, the enemy can smell it over fifteen meters away or it takes you till noon the next day to sweat it off. Most of the time we only use it on the bunker line at base camp.

Bob, all I've talked about is just day to day life in the bush. Not only do we have to fight the enemy but also the environment.

Hey babe, how are you today? You didn't think I was going to end this letter without expressing my love for you. Here goes; Bob I love you with all my heart, soul, and strength. If you were a mosquito I'd let your lips buzz all over my face and take an occasional bite. If you were a red ant you could put all the red marks on my neck you want. In other words, I'm completely yours!!!

Love,
Robt.

Trip to Phu Bai
05 Mar 1970
Dear Bob Jr,

Bob, as you know I love you more than anything in this world. And I hope that I have proven that to you over the past five years. But today I had an opportunity to demonstrate to others my love and devotion to you. And let me say this, "There was no wavering or second guessing about the decision I made." How does that old saying go "I was as serious as a heart attack."

Do you remember when I wrote and told you I would have to go to Phu Bai and clear up a finance problem with my pay? Well, today was the day. I went with two other

GI's from Camp Evans. We had no problems getting there. We hitched a ride on an army truck from Camp Evans all the way to Phu Bai.

After we completed our business we started looking for a ride back to Camp Evans. We found transportation but it was only going half way. However, we couldn't wait until we found the perfect ride because it was getting late and we did not want to get caught on the open highway at night. We only had M-16's and about five magazines a piece. So we took advantage of what was available at that moment. Half way to Camp Evans the truck turned off on a side road, dropped us of,f and kept going. So there we were, headed up the highway on foot. After about a mile and a half we approached a roadside village. Then all of a sudden three Vietnamese on scooters pulled up next to us. They offered to take us to Camp Evans for ten American Dollars apiece. I had my reservations but because it was getting late I went along with it. We had to take it because we were about twenty miles from Camp Evans. So, we got on the back of their scooters and headed north. We went about two miles, then all of a sudden they pulled of the highway onto a dirt road down an alley and into the back yard of a house. Then about six nice looking Vietnamese girls came out of the house. Those Vietnamese on the scooters took us to a whore house. The other two GI's didn't seem to mind it but I did. They went inside and took care of business while I stayed outside and waited. Bob, those people begged me to go inside and enjoy myself. Then the Vietnamese that I rode with said he wasn't going to take me the rest of the way if I didn't go inside and have a good time with the girls. Do you know the only way I was able to get him off my back was to give him money -- The price for one girl. After about an hour the other two GI's came out and we were headed back up the highway. We went about half a mile before they stopped and made us get off the scooters. There we were, stranded on Highway One in Vietnam with about three more hours before all Military Vehicles would have to be off the road. So, we started to jog. After about thirty minutes we heard a truck coming up behind us. It was a joint U.S. Army and South Vietnam Army Patrol. They stopped and asked us where we were going. We told them Camp Evans. They told us to hop on they were going that way and it was getting to dangerous for us to be out on the road. So, we got on the truck and made it to Camp Evans about thirty minutes before dark.

When we went to the guard station the MP's searched me and let me through. They searched the other two GI's and arrested them. They were in possession of marijuana. And guess where they bought it? At the whore house.

Bob, my love for you and a lot of silent prayer helped me through that situation. Love overcame the  temptation and prayer delivered me through the danger. And I did my part by staying "Focused on the Future". Bob, I'll be going back out to the field tomorrow. But tonight, I'll re-read a couple of (that's all I can keep at one time) your letters, think about you, read my Bible, and pray for us. I love you and I miss you so much.

Love,
Robt.

Camp Evans Military Base

07 Mar 1970 - 1

Dear Bob Jr,

Bob, how are you doing today? Do you have that cute little nose in your books?

Right now, I'm still at Camp Evans. Yesterday evening we tried to get out to the field but the weather didn't cooperate. It was extremely foggy in the mountains. We'll try again this afternoon.

Bob, could you do me a big favor. I'm going to send you a money order for about forty dollars so you can take Lisa and David and get them new shoes for Easter. But if you don't get the money before Easter, get the money out of the bank and replace it with the money order.

How is school coming along, babe? Are things getting better for you? By the way, how do you like Cheerleading? You don't mention it much in your letters. I know it's not like cheering at Attucks, but cheering on the College level has to be exciting. And I've said it before and I'll say it again, I'm very proud of you for making the team. When I talk about you to other's there is one thing I share that is always consistent, "She's a Ball State Cheerleader."

Bob, I love you so much that I wrote your mother and told her how much I love you. In addition, I told her that we are going to get married and that I'm going to take good care of you for the rest of your life.

Bob, I know we have over nine months to go but it will be over sooner than you think. We'll be together again and everybody will know it. Bob & Bob will be back together again setting the standard for love and relationships. Bob, I've told you how I'm getting through this and you have to do the same. Stay "FOCUSED ON THE FUTURE".

Love,
Robt.

Camp Evans Military Base
07 Mar 1970 - 2
Dear Bob Jr,
Bob, in my first letter today I forgot to mention the three letters I received from you yesterday. Babe, you made my day when I read in one of the letters that the Tigers of Crispus Attucks High School won their Boys High School Basketball Sectionals. I was so excited, yet kind of sad. I wasn't there to see it with you. You know we owe a lot to that school. That's where we spent part of our time falling in love with each other. That's where our identities changed to Bob & Bob. Even though we did not have one class together the entire four years, from our sophomore through our senior years we never failed to meet each other at my locker every period. You made it very convenient when you moved into it in the fall

Bobby Wright   Bobbie Hampton
                              1965

of 1965 and made it our locker. It was over that summer that we fell in love with each other. Some of our friends said we really got married, because after that summer we had forsaken all others. Bob not only did we have a very special love relationship we also had a very traditional courtship, "cheerleader and athlete." Even some of the teaching staff was impressed with the affection and devotion that we had for each another. Bob, please keep me informed of the Tigers performance in the Regionals. "Great memories."

Did you like your Easter cards? I hope so. I thought they were cute. Bob, since I'm going to reimburse you the money for Lisa and David's shoes, I want you to use some of that hundred dollars and buy yourself a new dress for Easter. And send me a picture of you wearing the dress. A lovely girl like you should look her best on Easter Sunday. If you want to match my outfit I'll be wearing green (smile).

Bob you're going into the last quarter of your sophomore year. I don't want you in any danger of getting behind. It will only delay our wedding and I know you're not having that.

Well, Babe, I've got to bring this letter to a close. Oh, by the way your letters are great. I don't know what I'd do without them. Keep up with your prayers. Just pray for me and love me and I'll be home safe and sound.

Love,
Robt.

Barbara Hampton
Co-Captain

A familiar sight to enemy
tacklers was the back of
Robert Wright.

Camp Evans Military Base

09 Mar 1970

Dear Bob Jr,

Bob, I'm not going back out to the field just yet. Since I'm already in Base Camp our Platoon Leader wants me to take on a project. Do you remember when I told you about Kit Carson Scouts? If you remember, I said they were once NVA Regulars or Viet Cong Guerrillas who surrendered and defected over to our side. In return, they get paid and their families are protected. We use them to walk point when we're in the field. Their primary responsibility is to detect any ambushes waiting us along the trail, including bunker sites and locating and disarming booby traps.

Every Scout has an American GI as his personal friend. And that's what my Platoon Leader wants me to be. I have to go through three weeks of tactics and language training with him, which I hear is no joke. We have to move to a separate part of the base to bunk and train with them. I'm supposed to be with him 24 hours a day. He's supposed to depend on me for everything. Even when we go back out

to the field I'm the one he'll go to for whatever he needs.
However, I will not be responsible for taking him to the
latrine (smile). My Platoon Leader wanted me to take on
this assignment because some Scouts are treated pretty
badly because of their prior affiliation with the enemy. Who
knows they may have even killed or wounded Americans in
the past. So, he selected me for the job because he knows
I'll treat him fairly. Don't worry, Babe, I'll be cautious. I'll
sleep with one eye open at all times. And I'll take good care
of him, so when we go back to the field he'll take good care
of me.

Well, Babe, are you still in love with me? You better
be, because I am and always will be in love with you. I
don't know what I'd do without you. As for me, there is no
such thing as love without you. I wish I could hug you right
now but my arms are just not long enough. But when we get
together again I'll hold you as gentle as a baby and yet so
close you'll think we became one. One thing I've learned
and learning since being over here is that being without
you is not what I call living. Every day we're not together
I'm in survival mode. Bob, I'm trying to make it from day-
to-day. But I know soon December will arrive and God will
reward us for our faithfulness. Just stay "Focused on the
Future". It will be here sooner than you think.

Love,
Robt.

Camp Evans Military Base
11 Mar 1970
Dear Bob Jr,
Bob, how was your day today? I had a very
productive day. I moved to my temporary location where

we'll be staying with our Scouts. I left most of my stuff back at Alfa Company.

We meet our Scouts today and we have some definite language barriers. My Scout's name is Neughn Den Vin. His English wasn't too bad, but it was broken up. He understands a lot of English words but he can't use them in phrases. The first thing I did was work through the interpreter to come up with a nick name for him. We agreed upon and he liked the nickname of "Slick." We agreed upon him calling me Bob. But after we spent some time together at lunch he added to my name "Number 1". The Vietnamese have a strange likeability scale. You're rated on a scale of 1 to 10. One being most likeable and ten being unlikeable. Here is the strange part. There are no middle ratings. You're either number one or number 10. And if they despise you you're "Number F_ _ _ ing 10" (excuse the language). Oh, and another thing, since we'll be training ten hours a day I don't have to go on Bunker Guard for the entire training period. However, we will have to take our Scouts out with us on Bunker Guard one night near the end of training and evaluate their performance. That will be a major part of the determination as to their readiness to serve in the field with GI's.

Well, I've got to go. Our training starts in about an hour. I'll keep you updated. I miss you so much!

Love,
Robt.

Camp Evans Military Base
16 Mar 1970
Dear Bob Jr,
Hi, Babe! What's going on with you? Are you taking care of yourself?

Here's some good news that I forgot to tell you about in my last letter. I received a promotion last week. My rank went from Private First Class to Specialist 4th Class. I'm a little proud of myself, and I hope you are too. Plus, the promotion comes with a raise. So, there will be a little more going into my Soldiers and Sailors savings account.

Bob, this morning I was very excited. Last night I called Alpha Company to check on whether or not I had received any mail. I was informed that there was one package and six letters in the mail box for me. After my ten o'clock class this morning I went straight over there and picked them up.

I feel pretty good this morning. It's probably because I went to Church Services last night. The sermon was good and I prayed for Alpha Company. They're operating somewhere close to the A Shaw Valley, one of the most dangerous regions in South Vietnam. And yesterday they had contact and suffered a few casualties. When I go get my mail today I'll find out more. Oh, by the way I know I haven't been mentioning it but I read my little Bible nearly every day. I almost have the Beatitudes in Matthew chapter five memorized. Do you remember my Grandmother Garvin gave me that Bible and made me promise to read it every day?

Bob, how are things at school? How's Glo and Rosie doing? Tell them I said "hello" and to take good care of you. Then when I get home I'll take over for good. Keep praying. If you get lonely just do as I do. Think of the day when we'll be back together. "Focus on the Future."

Remember a year may seem like a long time but eventually it will end. And then we'll be together again forever.

Love, Robt.

Camp Evans Military Base
18 Mar 1970
Dear Bob Jr,

Bob, today is Wednesday and all is well. If I were back in the World (home) I would call this hump day. Over here every day seems the same. Monday thru Sunday has no relevance. Well, maybe I should exclude Wednesday because if I were out in the field with my platoon I guess you could still call Wednesday hump day (see the point, smile).

Our training with our Scouts is going very well. They do pretty good on the field training part. Which shouldn't be a surprise to anyone. As a matter of fact, they taught us a few lessons on survival skills. The boring part is watching them learn English Grammar. It's kind of funny to. When they get mad they curse in Vietnamese. We don't know exactly what they are saying but we know foul language when we hear it. Bob, you may think I'm crazy for saying this but I'm kind of anxious to get Slick out in the field with the Platoon. His experience and knowledge can actually help save lives.

Yesterday he caught me reading my Bible and started asking me questions. He used to be a communist so he doesn't believe in God, so I focused on Jesus and his teachings of love and peace. My primary reference was the Beatitudes. I figure with him I better start with Jesus and work up to God. All those years Mom made us go to Sunday School is kind of paying off. I'm no Sunday School Teacher but I did go to Sunday School and listened to the

Teacher. So, we'll see what happens. I know I felt pretty good after explaining a few things to him.

Bob, Slick asked me did I "have girl". I said yes and showed him the bomb picture. He thought you were a "Number One Lady". You may not realize it, but you just got one heck of a compliment. Now I see why you're having problems at home, look at the impression you just had on Slick.

Well, that's my Vietnam report for the day. Now let me turn my attention to you. Bob, we're both surrounded by lots of people and yet we are both lonely. That's because we love each other so much. We miss sharing our love day-to-day, person-to-person and from heart-to-heart. Like I've said many times before when I was home we were inseparable. Bob, the Vietnamese have a name for the kind of relationship we have with each other. They would call us "same-same". In our case it speaks of our closeness or our oneness when we're together. For example; if we were walking down the street and someone called out, "Hey, Bob!" We would both turn around to respond. Or, if someone called Bob Sr. or Bob Jr., both of us would still turn around simultaneously. This time it would be to see who is calling the other, but we would still turn around together. Bob, I said all that to say I believe God has a plan for "us". It's not for me and it's not for you, it's for "us". So, we have to do our part and stay focused on His plan and not others (that includes the War in Vietnam). Stay "Focused, Babe".

Love,
Robt.

***P.S.** Bob, even though we're thousands of miles apart can you feel my love for you. I can feel your love for me. I can also feel your loneliness. But that's part of taking* *the bitter with the sweet. Life can seem bitter when you're separated from the one you love. We've been separated now for more than eight months and I have discovered something. The loneliness that I feel from being separated from you strengthens my love for you. It kind of follows that old saying, "Absence can make the heart grow fonder or absence can make the heart wander." The difference maker between the heart growing fonder or the heart wandering is "love". Bob, your letters help, your pictures help, but the key to overcoming the loneliness that I feel from not being with you, is the love that I have for you.*

Camp Evans Military Base
20 Mar 1970
Dear Bob Jr.
Hi, Bob, how are you getting along without Rosie. Losing your first roommate has to be an emotional setback for you. Rosie was even special to me because she was the one who rescued you from that rooming house you had to stay in when I took you to school for the first time. I remember you were so unhappy. I felt bad for you and mad at myself. I did not want to leave you in a situation where you were so unhappy. But a couple of weeks later it was Rosie to the rescue. And I'll always be indebted to her for that. Do you have any plans for a new roommate?
Well, Bob, I've got about six more days before Slick and I will be going out to the field. And I have mixed feelings about it. First, deep down inside I really don't want to go. Second, on the other hand I really need to get Slick out there so he can be a benefit to the Platoon. And third, me and a few other guys that came to the unit together have just been awarded the Combat Infantryman's Badge (CIB).

The CIB is only awarded to those who have actually participated in ground combat. Now, Bob, I have to fess up to you. So far in the short time I've been in country I have only told you about two direct encounters with enemy forces. I've actually been in five. Babe, I'm not, or should I say, "I can't tell you everything." But I'll keep you informed on a need to know basics. Some missions we may go out on and encounter nothing for ten days. Then there are other times when we'll go out on a mission and have contact with the enemy  *two-three days in a row. I don't want you worrying every day while I'm over here. But I do want you praying every day while I'm over here. If you do that, Babe, God will take care of the rest. I don't want any more on your little shoulders than what you can bear. Let me and God deal with the major stuff, you try and stay focused on your studies. For us grunts (nickname for Infantrymen) the CIB is a very prestigious award and an honor to wear.*

Bob, in your last letter you wanted to know if I were going to go on R&R (Rest & Relaxation). Well, I decided not to go on R&R. The only two options are Hawaii or Australia. Hawaii, although a good option, is out of the question. Only married couples (although we could probably put up a good argument why we should be considered) can go there. And I don't think your mother will be in favor of you traveling to and from Australia alone. Nor would I. Besides I can't picture Australia as a very romantic rest stop for us. So that means more than likely I won't be going on R&R. Hopefully they'll tack those days onto my leave time after Vietnam. Hopefully that

*will put me home through Christmas and New Year's. I
hope, I hope, I hope.*

*Bob, thanks for sending a picture in your last letter. It
really helped to get me out of a rut. Right now, I feel like a
parasite. Emotionally I'm living off your letters and the
love you express through them. But I'm a very rare
Parasite because as I'm being renewed I'm sending my
love to you. Bob, I hope my letters are conveying the love
and devotion that I have for you. And my intent is not for
them to just cheer you up. But I'm hoping that they literally
sweep you off your feet and take you to a destination where
I am eagerly awaiting. Or since this is not an Alice In
Wonderland movie I'll settle for just an, "I love you too,
Robert." And I'll respond by saying "I love you more and
more each and every day" regardless of where we are.*

Love,
Robt.

Camp Evans Military Base

23 Mar 1970
Dear Bob Jr,

*It's me again. Writing to let you know what I've been
doing the past three days and of course writing to let you
know how much I love you.*

*Bob, what happened to the Tigers. I heard about them
losing in the State Semi-Finals. I was really looking
forward to them going all the way. But we both know how
tough Indiana High School Basketball is.*

*Tell Sylvia I miss her to. And yes, I remember how
much we wrestled all the time. And I remembered when
your mother got on us for wrestling too much. And don't
think I have forgotten the times you felt sorry for Sylvia and*

110

Bob Jr. and Sylvia

joined in and you both jumped on me together. Those were the good old days that gave rise to better days. And eventually you didn't like your sister messing with me all the time and taking up my attention because you wanted all my attention for yourself. Then that's when the good old days got better. A whole lot better. You became very selfish. You wanted me all to yourself. I couldn't get enough of you. I wanted more and more and more. I know your Mother was tired of seeing me every evening Monday thru Sunday. But as long as you wanted to see me I was willing to chance it. Although, if I can remember she did send me home a couple of times. Then she got mad because as soon as I got home we would get on the phone and tie it up. Sometimes your mother would say "this wasn't natural" (referring to us being together so much). All we could say about that was, "You're right, it's not natural."

Now on the war front, for the past two days we had to take the Scouts out for more field training before we go to the field to join the rest of our units.

My platoon has constantly been on the move the past week. I'm hearing rumors they may be coming

Nollie Jean Hampton (Bob Jr's Mother)

back to base camp soon to rest up before a big offensive

that is in the works. Other than that, there hasn't been any bad news. One of the guys from my platoon came in from the field today to get ready to go on R&R. We had our laughs and then he started to tease me about being in the rear (Base Camp) for so long. I reminded him that I did not volunteer for this assignment. I was chosen without the opportunity to express any objection. Then we laughed it off and talked about his R&R.

Before he took off to go to Battalion to process I introduced him to Slick. I told him Slick was going to be our new scout for the platoon. And to my surprise he was not very warm towards Slick. I did not know what to think. Bob, I was caught off guard. I know Slick sensed it too. Maybe I shouldn't have given him the nickname "Slick." Maybe I should have named him "Honest Abe" or something. So, I told Slick to go and get ready for chow and meet me by the Mess Hall. Then I went to the Sergeant Major and told him what had just happened. He said to me, "What did you expect?" To some guys you're going to bring the enemy right into the camp and they won't trust Slick until there's a situation where he saves their butts. There's going to be a trust issue at the start. And that's why you were selected for this assignment. Your Platoon Leader figured you were the best person in his unit to make this work. Wow, here I've been kind of anxious to get Slick out in the field and start working with the guys, but now I see the whole picture. If they don't trust him then they'll never accept him. And the Sergeant Major had given me the answer in his own elegant way (save their butts). Slick had to prove himself to them. And that all depends on opportunities.

Now I see why they say War is hell. It's not just bang-bang-shoot-em-up. They didn't teach relationship building in AIT or Scout Training. Well, I'll figure it out. I'll start out by leading by example and then wait and see where I need to go from there.

Well, Babe, I hope you're not as discouraged as I am right now. The only relationship building I've been successful at is with you. Our relationship has grown from interest to fondness to dating to courtship to being madly in love. Now that's relationship building there (laugh). And I have enjoyed and been blessed by every stage of it. I love you, Bob.

Love,
Robt.

Camp Evans Military Base

26 Mar 1970
Dear Bob Jr,
How is my future wife getting along? Well, I'm back in the company area. I moved back last night. Slick and I will be going out to the field the day after tomorrow. That will be Saturday. Bob, when I woke up this morning I ran into two guys that were leaving to go home today. Bob, they were so happy. At that moment, all I could think of was December-December-December and Bob-Bob-Bob. Like the Preacher always says, "As sure as the sun comes up in the east and goes down in the west." All we have to do is

count about 257 more sun rises and sunsets and I'll be on my way home.

Bob, I got a letter from Sylvia today along with her senior picture. She's grown into a very attractive young lady, but she is still crazy. She ended her letter by saying "Well, Robt., I'll let you go now. You probably have to use the latrine or something." And she sent the letter with a picture of Pepe's Paw. Like I said, cute and crazy.

Well, Babe, I've got to run. I have to take Slick over to supply and get him equipped for the field. He's kind of excited about it. He's especially excited about wearing the Screaming Eagle Patch.

Right now, looking at one of your pictures and you know what? You're the cutest thing under the Sun. You have just brightened up my day. Now I see why you don't have to wear makeup. It's because you have love painted all over your face. I love you and I think about you all the time. Night and day.

Love,
Robt.

Camp Evans Military Base
01 Apr 1970
Dear Bob Jr,

First of all, I want to comment on how nice you looked in the black and white dress. You were just down right gorgeous. You looked like a very lovely model. And just think you belong to me. I'll have you all to myself I will keep that picture very close.

Bob, I have some promising news. The other day I talked with the Officer in charge of Battalion Communications and he said he would be glad to hire me if I could get a transfer from Alfa Company. He indicated I *would be a great fit for his unit. I have a secondary MOS of 36-KILO (Telephone Wireman) as a result of working at Indiana Bell. And because of my combat experience I would be ideal for installing communication systems on fire bases. But the bottom line is, the final decision will be up to the Company Commander of Alfa Company. And right now, I'm having problems making it happen. But don't worry I won't give up. If I can make this happen I'll have a rear job and won't be out in the field on search and destroy missions. I'll work on it from this end and you pray from your end and we'll see how it works out. I'm sure God is in the plan. Don't worry I'll keep you informed.*

Bob, how are things with you? Do you miss me? I certainly miss you. What are you taking in school this quarter? Are you still behind in credits? If so what are your plans for getting caught up? I hope you will not have to go to summer school. Come June "72" I want you to be done with everything.

As far me the main issue here is this unmerciful hot weather. After I take a cold shower I still sweat. And just think, this is just the beginning of the hot season. Sorry I haven't been able to write as much lately. For the past few nights I've been on bunker guard.

Well, be good and take care of yourself. Always know that you're on my mind and my heart. I love you and yes, I'm "Focused on the Future".

Love,
Robt.

I'll keep working on that rear job. If I can get it I know that will take a lot of pressure off of you and Mom.

Camp Evans Military Base

03 Apr 1970
Dear Bob Jr,

Bob, I just finished reading a very inspiring letter from you today. Your letters are always encouraging. They lift me up emotionally, they give me hope and most of all they assure me of your love for me. They keep me inspired so I can be an encouragement to you. You see why we're so important to each other. We keep each other going. When two people love each other like we do they develop a sense of reciprocal responsibility. In other words, the quality of our individual lives is based on what we sow into each other's lives. The comfort and encouragement that I receive from your letters is what I try to incorporate in the letters I write to you. That's what makes us so vital to one another.

Bob, I'm going back to the field tomorrow. Then on the fifth the whole Battalion is going to Eagle Beach for rest and relaxation. Eagle Beach is a recreational center located on a small beach in the South China Sea about six miles east of Hue. It's three days of doing whatever you want to do; hang out on the beach, go to the theater, play sports, and at night go to the USO shows. I'll write you from there.

Bob, outside of being lonely I'm doing pretty good. Of course, I have to keep my spirit up in order to keep your spirit up. I think about you so much that whenever my close friend sees me in deep thought he asks me, "How's Bob Jr.?" Isn't that crazy!

Sometimes he calls me a "love-sick Zombie". And the only thing that gets me out of that state is when we're in the field on a mission. So, I want to reemphasize that you're always on my mind and I love you very much.

Bob, I know we're very lonely for each other. But once you're in my arms again our memories of this year will become reminders of how much we love each other, how much we need each other, and how miserable we are when we're separated from each other. Plus, we've never stopped being Bob & Bob, so when this is over people will again see Bob & Bob.

Bob would you believe I've grown an inch since I've been in the Service. So that means you'll have to tip toe a little higher when I take you in my arms for a kiss. And I'm sure you won't mind. Well, I've got to run. Thinking of you at all times and loving you all the time.

Love,
Robt.

Eagle Beach, South China Sea
06 Apr 1970
Dear Bob Jr,
Bob, I'm writing this letter from Eagle Beach. This is our second day of supposedly a three day stay but it's going to be cut short. We're leaving here tomorrow morning and going straight to the field on a 90-day mission. Something hot is coming down. Slick is going to get on the Choppers at Camp Evans and meet us here at Eagle Beach.

Now, enough of that, let me tell you about Eagle Beach. It is wonderful. We were totally free to rest and relax. Everything was free. Beer is the only alcohol

allowed. There was plenty of beer and sodas, they
barbequed steaks it was great. And they had three USO
Shows every day. It was kind of strange hearing Motown
Songs sung in Vietnamese accents but we didn't care. The
only act I gave them a bad grade on was The Temptations.
They didn't sound bad but the choreography let's say was
less than acceptable. But otherwise they were great. I spent
most of my time playing beach volleyball, watching the
USO Shows, and relaxing on the beach. There was plenty
of running hot water all day (hot showers) and a modern
mess hall. And guess what!! No bugs. It's going to be hard
leaving this place tomorrow. Especially when we have to
get up at 5 A.M. We have to be in full combat gear and
ready to board the Helicopters at 7 A.M.

Guess who I was thinking about when I was relaxing
on the beach? You, You
and You!! As a matter of
fact, there were several of
you dancing around my
beach chair in bathing
suits. I had sunglasses to
protect my eyes from
being blinded by all that
beauty and I had a big
grin on my face enjoying
all that beauty. I'll take
you in a bathing suit over

a cheerleading uniform any day. Yeah Bob, you didn't
know it but you spent two whole days with me on the beach.
We did get to go on R&R together after all.

Well, Babe, here's the update on that rear job. The
Company Commander said if I'll give him two more
months in the field, then he'll release me to take that job. I

told him that was fair. Now I have to see if the Communications Shop can live with that time frame. I'll keep you informed. I've got to go. I think the Supremes are going to perform the last show tonight. Then I've got to hit the sack. Remember we have an early start tomorrow. Maybe when I get out of the service you and I will get a chance to see the Temptations and Supremes. I love you, and you were hot in that bathing suit.

Love,
Robt.

Field Mission   (Search and Destroy)
07 Apr 1970
Dear Bob Jr,

Bob, this will be a letter written in haste. By dusk everybody has to be alert and ready for anything. This morning shortly after we left Eagle Beach everything went from calm to chaos. When we got close to the designated LZ for our drop off we started receiving small arms fire from the ground. Hearing those bullets hitting the Medal frame of the Helicopter was very frightening at first. The door gunner yelled at us to move back toward the center of the Helicopter out of the door openings. After about five minutes of taking evasive action my Platoon Leader told (yelled) me that we were headed to an alternate LZ and that me and my Scout would lead the Platoon off the LZ. Then, all of a sudden we started receiving small arms fire again. We were told that the Helicopters will not touch ground and we would have to jump out at four feet. The problem with that was our rucksacks were full of gear, ammo, and water (about 70 lbs.).

As the Helicopters began their final approach to the LZ the Door Gunners provided cover fire with their M-60 Machine Guns. As we got closer to the LZ the terrain looked familiar to me. Then I recognized the LZ as one that I had helped to cut a few weeks ago.

When we descended to four feet above the ground the Door Gunner gave us the signal to go and we jumped out of the first Helicopter safe and sound (no one shot, no broken ankles). But we had to move quickly because other Helicopters were right behind us with the rest of the Platoon and subsequently the rest of the Company. The Lieutenant (Platoon Leader) ordered us to "move out" and pointed to a trail that leads off the LZ through the bush.

Right away Slick and I looked at each other and knew that was not a safe way to go. So, I quickly informed the Lieutenant of the situation and directed him in another direction off the LZ. Slick and I then went back up to the top of the LZ to direct the rest of the company off the LZ  *avoiding that trail. After the whole Company had safely landed I went back to the Lieutenant to explain why it was best to avoid the trail. I explained to him that I was on the team that cut the LZ and we did not cut any trails through the bush leading off the LZ. He understood and later ordered Slick and myself to check out the trail. We uncovered two booby traps. The type of booby traps Slick disarmed would have killed twelve to fifteen people. Slick and I earned a little respect today. The Platoon then moved away from the LZ and we set up our night defensive perimeter.*

Bob, I didn't want to tell you all this but I want you to have some idea what we may encounter on any given day. I have to stop writing now. I've got to eat something (c-rations) before we set up our guard rotations tonight. We probably won't get much sleep tonight. I love you and I need your prayers.

Love,
Robt.

Field Mission (Search and Destroy)

10 Apr 1970 - 1
Dear Bob Jr,
Bob, how is the girl of my dreams getting along? You're probably sleeping right now. I hope you're dreaming about me. Last night I thought about you before I fell off to sleep. I thought about when we said goodbye before I left for Vietnam. There we were standing in front of Wilson Hall sharing our goodbyes. To me it felt like half of me was dying. And I'll never forget our goodbye kiss. The softness of your lips, the sweetness of your mouth mixed with the taste of your tears and the smell of your perfume. When I return I want to experience all of that only this time that half of me that died will be alive again. Bob, do you remember all those Friday nights we spent at your house watching scary movies in the den? One movie we watched many times over was the Frankenstein movie starring Gene Wilder. Do you remember the most well-known line from that movie, "He's Alive, He's Alive"? When I see you

again I'll be saying something very similar, "I'm Alive, I'm Alive."

We had a quiet night last night but from what I hear Charlie Company had one extraordinary night. One of their men while pulling his guard shift was attacked by a tiger. Can you believe that? He survived, but I hear he had deep lacerations to his face. Bob, Charlie Company is operating only a mile from us. Now when we pull guard at night we'll have to be extra careful while we're operating in this area. Wow and I thought the mosquitoes were bad.

Bob, tomorrow I may have to return to Camp Evans. Slick is very sick. He has a high fever and the only thing he'll tell us is that "he needs to see Doctor". Our Medic has given him aspirin but without Slick being more specific there's nothing else he can do for him in the field. I hope we can get him back there tonight. Because if we have to move out tomorrow, I don't think he will be able to.

Well, I've got to go. I think there're trying to decide what to do with Slick. If they can get a Chopper we'll have to go back to the same LZ we came in on. That can be a little dangerous for a small patrol. I'll let you know. I love you very much!!!

Love, Robt.
Camp Evans Military Base
10 Apr 1970 - 2
Dear Bob Jr,

Bob, we made it to Camp Evans today. However, it was a hairy trip back to the LZ. We went slow and very cautious. The Helicopter arrived at the same time as we did. We timed it just right.

When we arrived at Camp Evans, I took Slick to the Aide Station right away. They took him in and told me they would let us know something tomorrow. So I gave Slick a thumbs-up and a pat on the shoulder and then headed for the company area to report in. Afterwards I went to the Mess Hall and they gave me something to eat. Then I went and got some clean clothes, took a shower, and headed to the Battalion Day Room for tonight's movie.

Tonight they showed our favorite movie, Romeo and Juliet. I enjoyed it but you know who I was thinking about throughout the movie, Roberto and Barbara-et. All jokes aside, Bob, you were definitely on my mind. You're the one I love and you're the one I plan to marry. It's getting late and I don't know what's on the agenda for tomorrow.

Love,
Robt.

Camp Evans Military Base
12 Apr 1970
Dear Bob Jr,

Well, Bob, I received the medical report on Slick this morning. His blood test has revealed that he has an advanced case of Syphilis. A single shot of penicillin won't be enough; he will need more intense treatment and care. That means he won't be going back to the field with me tomorrow. The sad part is Slick has a wife and kids. I really feel sorry for him and his family. And I think he would have been a great Scout.

Tomorrow I'll be going back to the field. In one sense, I'm not looking forward to it because of the obvious reasons and this unbearable heat. It hasn't rained in a week and a half. For the guys in the field that means conserving water and limiting their activity. They don't want anyone to have a heat stroke and have to Medevac them out. That would give away their position. On the other hand, I'm ready to go back to the field. I had a conversation with the Commo Chief this morning. I informed him of the stipulation set forth by my Company Commander that he would release me only after I serve two more months in the field. Bob, the Commo Chief had no problem with that timeline because he has two men going home around that same timeframe. So, he committed to issuing the transfer paperwork at the proper time. That means I've got to get this two-month time clock ticking. Another issue I've got to deal with is, because of the training I received with Slick, I'll probably be walking point a lot. But if there's anything that I have learned in this man's Army over the past nine months is "You have to take the bitter with the sweet." That's also part of the maturing process of growing from a boy to a man.

Bob, I also think that the maturing process applies to relationships as well. I think our relationship has matured, especially in the areas of faithfulness, devotion, and commitment. Here we are at the ages of 19 and 20 and our relationship has grown far from just hugging and kissing. We have been faithful to one another in that despite all the distractions; we have maintained our love for each other. We have been devoted to one another by remaining "focused on our future" together. We have remained committed to one another by our efforts to encourage and strengthen each other through this period of separation. Bob, I will always love you. I can make that declaration today, because the relationship that we have developed together over the past four years will be a strong foundation for our love in the future.

Love,

Robt.

Field Mission (Search and Destroy)
13 Apr 1970
Dear Bob Jr,

Bob, when I wrote you yesterday I forgot to let you know that I did make it to one of the Church Services. Whenever I'm in the rear one of my priorities is to attend a church service. Now that I'm back out in the field it will probably be awhile before I get a chance to attend.

Yes, I'm back in the field, but with a different outlook. My focus is on a two-month window in the field rather than eight months. But I won't let that go to my head. Regardless of how much time I have left in the field I'll take each day one day at a time.

When I arrived to the field and got off the Chopper I was immediately told to report to my Platoon Leader. He gave me an over view of our mission for the next few days and informed me that I was selected to walk point most of the time. He also informed me that Battalion is restricting our letter writing to two letters a week. Because of our current mission they want us to be focused more on Charlie (the enemy) and less on what's happening back home. In addition, resupply days will be every five days instead of every three. They don't want the Helicopters giving away our positions as frequently.

Bob, I got a letter from Michael the other day and he was telling me David was misbehaving. Is that true, do you know what's going on?

Well, we didn't do any humping today; we kind of just stayed in place. We'll probably send out a couple of Ambush Patrols tonight. Since I have to walk point tomorrow I don't have to worry about that. I'll need to be

well-rested so I'll be alert tomorrow. We'll pick up the
Ambush Patrols when we move out in the morning.

Well, I have to end this letter. It will be awhile before
you get it, so I hope you won't be alarmed. But always
remember my love for you is timeless so when you do get
this letter I'll still be very much in love with you.

Love,
Robt

Field Mission (Search and Destroy)
18 Apr 1970
Dear Bob Jr,

Hi, Bob, well, I'm writing you on a very hot Saturday
evening. We are through humping for the day and setting
up our night defensive perimeter (NDP). We are
somewhere in the area of Fire Base Ripcord. This week
wasn't too bad. Although, we did have contact with the
NVA on two occasions. During both incidents, I was
walking point.

The first incident happened around noon on
Wednesday. We were on a mountain ridge and we heard
movement on our right flank. After we identified that the
movement was not friendly forces we opened fire. They
returned fire with small arms (AK-47's). After about five
minutes of engagement we saturated the area with M-79
fire (grenades). Enemy contact broke off and we did a
sweep of the area. We found two dead enemy soldiers and

three separate blood trails. All we sustained were two minor injuries.

However, yesterday we were not as fortunate; we were on our mission when we were attacked from the rear. Since we were on high ground we were able to repel their attack. Unfortunately, we sustained  *casualties. We had one dead and two wounded. Not a good day at all. Our main focus now was to get our casualties to an LZ for immediate extraction. The LZ was 200-meters away. We made it to the LZ without incident. Within ten minutes of our arrival the Medevac Chopper arrived escorted by a Cobra Gunship. We got our casualties loaded and then met up with the Platoon and proceeded on our mission.*

Bob, when you talk to the brothers at Ball State make sure they understand and appreciate the opportunity they have. A lot of them have not been drafted because of their school deferments. So they should take full advantage of that opportunity by making sure their main focus is getting a good education, and not just using college to dodge the draft. And let me add this, being in the Army and serving in Vietnam has been an educational process for us also. The difference is, if we don't stay focused, the consequences are a lot more painful. And, in some cases, deadly.

Well, I better move to my position for the night and get my claymore (mine) set out. Hopefully I'll get a few minutes of quiet time so I can re-read your last letter. Especially the part where you tell me how much you miss me and love me. It's times like these that your words mean so much to me.

Love,
Robt.

Field Mission (Search and Destroy)
22 Apr 1970
Dear Bob Jr,

Well, Babe, how is your day going today? Since I'm writing this on a Wednesday other than going to class what is your normal Wednesday routine. Today is re-supply day for us. Re-supply is okay because we get food, cigarettes, candy, writing paper and envelopes, magazines, ammunition, clean dry socks, and best of all MAIL. So hopefully I'll be reading a letter from you today. Now the negative aspect of re-supply day is the next day when we have to move out and we have to put on rucksacks that will be three times heavier than normal. Since this is re-supply day, the Helicopters expose our position so we'll probably have to move out. Hopefully we won't have to move too far.

Bob, we're getting close to the end of April. That's four and a half months. We're getting closer to the half-way mark. Although I still miss you very much I look forward to everyday that we're apart because it's a day closer to us being together again. Oh, Happy Days!

Love,
Robt.

23 Apr – 15 Jun 70
No Letters Found for This Period

Fire Base O'Reilly (Central Highlands)
16 Jun 1970
Dear Bob Jr,
Bob, I am writing to you this evening literally covered in mud. Last night our Squad Leader came to each of us individually and informed us that we have to be packed up, ready to move out by 5A.M., and at the LZ by 5:30A.M. We (Alpha Company) are going to take over Fire Base O'Reilly from Delta Company. We will be there for approximately two to three weeks. Our responsibility will be: (1) provide security for the Artillery Battery and the Mortar Crews operating on the fire base, and (2) refortifying the fire base.

Bob, when we arrived to the Fire Base this morning we were immediately broken down into two-man teams and taken to designated positions that we would be responsible for defending. And Bob, this is a very <u>tall</u> <u>mountain</u>. Our objective for today was to dig a foxhole big enough and deep enough for two to fight from and live in. Tomorrow when we get the materials we need we will cover the tops, reinforce with sandbags thus changing our fighting positions into bunkers. Then on a daily basis we'll improve and extend the killing zone all the way to the bottom of the mountain.

We started digging our foxholes around 8A.M. and most of us were done by 11A.M. Then it happened; Bob, all of a sudden, the storm clouds rolled in, it got dark, and then the deluge. It rained so hard equipment and materials were being washed down the side of the mountain. One of the dangers that plague fire bases are storms. Those nice dry foxholes we had just dug were now filled to the top and running over with water, or shall I say mud. So we went from digging foxholes to bailing water out of foxholes. The disgusting part about all this is that when the sun comes out in two hours the foxholes will be bone dry. And our fatigues will be dry but muddy, "all night". So, for the rest of the day we focused our attention on finishing our foxholes and getting them ready so we'll have a safe place to sleep and defend our positions. This included filling and stacking sand bags. Bob, it was a hot and miserable day. And we were also concerned about snipers. Working out in the open like that made us very susceptible to sniper fire. We were sitting ducks for any sniper 500-meters and out. So we worked with reckless abandon. To combat the heat, we took needed breaks and drank plenty of water. Bob, we drank so much water that at the end of the day our Company Commander requested and we receive a special re-supply of fresh water. We finished our foxholes and prepared for the evening. We secured our weapons in the foxholes along with ammunition and firing devices for our claymores and other enemy deterrent surprises. We ate chow (C-Rations), settled in our foxholes, and waited for night fall. We used this time for ourselves. We read books

(including Bibles), listened to music (w/earphones), and wrote letters like I'm doing right now.

Bob, this is when I miss you the most. This is when I reflect on every thought and memory I have of you. Your smile, your soft lips, your tender kisses, the sound of your voice, the smell of your perfume, and I'm going to say it, "your sexiness". Some would ask why torture myself by thinking about those things when I still have seven months to go on my tour in Vietnam. Well, I don't view them as things I don't have. I view them as rewards that I will receive once I finish my tour. Bob, in December you'll be my reward for remaining faithful to you and to God. Yes, I miss you now but soon (and very soon) we'll be together again.

Love, Robt.

Oh, I forgot the very last thing we have to do this evening is to stand (or sit) at the front of our foxholes and align our fields of fire with the foxholes to left and to the right. This is so that if we're attacked we'll have connecting fields of fire. That means when we shoot back

we won't have any dead zones that the enemy can use to penetrate our defenses.

Fire Base O'Reilly (Central Highlands)

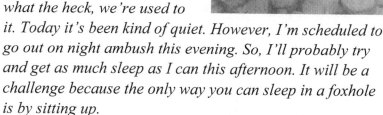

18 Jun 1970

Dear Bob Jr,

Well, Bob, we survived our occupation of the Fire Base the other day. However, we still haven't received a change of clothes yet. But what the heck, we're used to it. Today it's been kind of quiet. However, I'm scheduled to go out on night ambush this evening. So, I'll probably try and get as much sleep as I can this afternoon. It will be a challenge because the only way you can sleep in a foxhole is by sitting up.

Yesterday we had to deal with a sniper. But no one was hurt and we finally flushed out his location and took care of him with Artillery. While I'm on the subject of Artillery; Bob, do you remember how you always complained about people in the neighborhood shooting off fireworks after the 4th of July? Well, imagine that level of noise magnified by one thousand. That's how loud it is on a fire base at night. The Artillery Batteries are firing missions for about four hours every night. And the Mortar Crews are at it "off" and "on" during the day. So much for a peaceful night's sleep or mid-day nap. Bob, I remember those Saturday nights going over to your house after I got off work. We would be watching T.V. in the den and you would put a pillow in your lap and I would lean over and lay my head down on it and fall sound asleep. It didn't last long but it was very peaceful. I remember sometimes you would fall asleep too and the only thing that woke us up was the sound from the test pattern on the television after all the station programming had gone off. Then I would have to slip out of your house without waking up your mother. Those were the good old days. But don't worry I'm sure that after we're married we'll experience lots of those kinds of moments again. Only the conditions will be a little different. I won't have to get up and leave and there won't be a pillow between me and thee (smile).

Stay "Focused on our Future" and I'll do my very best to make it happen. I miss being with you, and I'm miserable being without you.

Love,
Robt.

19 Jun – 06 Jul 70
No Letters Found for This Period

Camp Evans Military Base
07 Jul 1970
Dear Bob Jr,
I'm back at Camp Evans because of an incident that happened last night. I was on guard standing in my foxhole scanning the area with the night vision scope, when all of a

sudden there was an explosion at the bottom of the fire base and the next thing I knew I was lying on the ground looking up at the stars. My foxhole partner woke up startled wondering what had happen. He asked me if I was okay and I responded, "I think so." Then all of a sudden, I felt this burning sensation coming from my left elbow. When I grabbed my elbow, I discovered that I had been hit. There was blood all over my arm. I was bleeding badly. My Squad Leader made his way over to our position and immediately escorted me over to the Aid Station. It is very difficult walking on the side of a mountain with your hands and arms pre-occupied. After the Medics stopped the bleeding and examined my wound they discovered that I had been hit by a piece of shrapnel. They decided that it was in too deep and too close to a major nerve to attempt to remove it in the field. They also told me that because I was looking through the night scope that the position of my elbow most likely shielded my heart from the path of the shrapnel. "God is good all the time and all the time God is good." So, they bandaged it up for the night and gave me some pain killers to help ease the pain. It bled so much off and on that I had to return to the Medics twice overnight to have it re-bandaged. Early this morning my Platoon Leader came to my foxhole and informed me that the shrapnel that hit me came from friendly fire. One of the artillery rounds fired from the fire base fell short and exploded dangerously close to our perimeter. Then he proceeded to inform me that because my wound was caused by friendly fire he would not be recommending me for a Purple Heart. Bob, I was kind of offended by that statement. The last thing I had on my mind was the Purple Heart. My response was simply, "I fully understand, Sir."

And I left it at that. Then they gathered up my gear and put me on the early flight to Camp Evans.

When I arrived at base camp I reported directly to Top (Sergeant Major) and then directly to the Aid Station. When I arrived at the Aid Station the Doctors knew all about my situation and started their examination immediately. I didn't get worried until they decided to take X-Rays. After the examination, they shared with me their decision. I was hit by a small piece of shrapnel that is lodged very close to a major nerve. The reason why it caused so much bleeding was the shrapnel sliced through my arm and hit two small blood vessels. To remove it could risk damage to the nerve. So, they recommended, because of its small size, that the shrapnel be left in my arm and that scar tissue will grow around it and shield it from the body. After the wound heals the most discomfort I should feel is occasional itching. And in time that will go away. They asked me how much service time will I have left after my tour in Vietnam. I told them seven and a half months. They said if I had any problems stateside to just go to the Base Hospital and they'll have my medical history. Then they put a temporary waterproof bandage on my wound and sent me to get some clean clothes and take a shower. After taking a <u>hot</u> <u>shower</u> and putting on <u>clean</u> <u>clothes</u> I felt human again. When I returned to the Aid Station they dressed my wound with a permanent bandage and put me on a seven-day profile. They did not want me doing anything that would cause excessive sweating to infect the wound. Then I said to myself, "Is he kidding, in Vietnam turning over in bed at night can cause excessive sweating." Before I left they wrote out the profile and added to it that they needed to see *me for the next seven days to change the bandage and monitor the status of the wound.*

When I returned to the company area and gave the profile to Top he looked at me with one eye open and one eye closed. Bob, it was as if he was sizing me up. Then he asked me how much schooling I had. I told him I had a High School Education. Then he asked me did I have a particular field of study. I said, "Yes, Business Administration." His  *response was, "Outstanding." Then he told me that he had a lot of extra filing that he needed done and that he was looking for someone he could rely on to do it right. I told him I could handle that. His response was, "We'll see."*

Bob, the bottom line is I'm okay. You still have "all" your man and we're now past the halfway mark with five and a half months to go. God is faithful. If we would just keep praying and remain "focused" we'll get through this. I miss you, need you, want you, thinking about you, and I love you very much. Oh, Bob, please share all of this with my mother.

Love,
Robt.

Camp Evans Military Base

10 Jul 1970

Dear Bob Jr,

Bob, how are you today? How did your work day go? Has the weather turned hot and miserable yet? I would ask you what the temperature is but I won't. Because whatever it is when I compare it with what it is here I'm sorry but I won't have a lot of sympathy for you. I got your last letter and I will agree with you that being at home with your family and neighborhood friends are perfect antidotes to the boredom and loneliness of summer school.

Well, Bob, I can't hold it off any longer. My transfer orders came through today. Effective July 20th I'll no longer be in Alfa Company. I've been reassigned to the Battalion Communications Group. I wish I could see the smile on your face and the gleam in your eyes right now. On one hand, I am very happy because to some degree I'll be out of harm's way, which will take a lot of pressure off all of us. On the other hand, from the Communications Shack I can monitor the radios and keep up with the activities of Alfa Company.

Next week, I'll be meeting with the Commo Chief to go over my duties and responsibilities. He has already warned me that my main responsibilities at times will require sixteen-hour work days. Bob, that will be no problem at all. When I was out in the field we were on duty 24-hours a day.

Bob, all I can do right now is to thank you and Mom and the family for all your prayers and to "Thank God" for answering them. As they say in Church, "He's a mighty good God, yes, he is, yes he is."

137

Since you gave my mom the unpleasant news about me getting wounded, I'll give you the honors of sharing with her this good news. Well, I have to get to chow before all the good portions are gone. Then I have to get back on that filing project for the Sergeant Major. Bob, I've noticed from your letters that you've been worrying about me a lot. I think this good news will relieve some of that worry. But don't stop praying. I still need your love and your prayers. "STAY FOCUSED."

Love,
Robt.

Camp Evans Military Base
14 Jul 1970
Dear Bob Jr,

I am anxiously awaiting your response to the news of my transfer to the Battalion Communication's Group. I can't wait for you to share with me every thought and emotional outburst you and Mom had. I want to hear it all.

I met with the Commo Chief today and he laid out all the different duties and responsibilities I will have. At night, I'll be in the rotation for Bunker Guard and Switchboard Operator. During the day, I will be the primary Jeep Driver for the Commo Shop. I'll either be using the Jeep for repairing wiring problems anywhere on base or driving Communication's Personnel around the base to deliver or repair radio or telephone equipment. At all times, I will be required to carry my M-16. I will also be responsible for their security.

Bob, I'm going to be working a lot of hours and double shifts within a 24-hour period and I'll have to sleep when I can. So that means my letter writing may drop off a little. But don't worry, you will not be neglected. I'll write you while setting in the rest room if it comes to that (just kidding). I'm looking forward to this new assignment and will do whatever they need me to do. I've heard of other's who transferred from the field for similar opportunities who did not live up to expectations and as a result they were sent back to the field. Although I will not be in a direct combat role, I am still in a combat zone, asked to perform a very important mission, and I'll do it to the best of my ability. I also see this opportunity as a blessing that God had waiting or should I say "prepared" for me. Bob, all this kind of lines up with what the Pastor preached about at church Sunday when he said, "Every good and perfect gift comes from the Lord." Well, let me get back to work on Alfa Company's files. I promised the Sergeant Major that I will have them squared away (completed) before I leave.

Bob, I feel so blessed getting this opportunity and by having a fiancée who not only loves me but who also prays for me. Including my mom and my family. What a turn of events these past few weeks. I hope you think about me all day as I will be thinking about you all day.

Love,
Robt.

Camp Evans Military Base (Communications Shop)
20 Jul 1970
Dear Bob Jr,
Bob, this was my first day on my new assignment. I feel a little odd not being a part of Alfa Company any more.

But I'm not feeling guilty or nothing like that I just know firsthand what those guys have to go through. In a way of showing my support, I promised one of my friends that I would make sure that he gets a current issue of Sports Illustrated every month. He's crazy about sports. I even made a deal with a checkout clerk at the PX to hold back a copy for me soon as they come in.

This morning I went to the Motor Pool today to go over the procedures for checking out and maintenance of the Jeep assigned to the Commo Shop. When I pursued this transfer to the Commo Shop I had no idea driving a  Jeep would be part of my overall responsibility. This along with my other responsibilities will keep me quite busy. And that's a good thing because the busier I am the faster the time goes.

Bob, speaking of time going by do you realize that we have less than five months to go. Wow! It won't be long before we're together again. That is one event that I'm really looking forward to. Right now, it seems so unreal but at the same time every day that goes by it's becoming more of a reality. Bob, I've even notice in your most recent letters a certain sense of excitement and expectation. Your words reveal a mood of happiness rather than loneliness. And the thoughts that you reveal are more focused on the joys that await us rather than the pain of the present. Even when I look at your pictures I see in them something *different. Not someone that I left behind but someone I'll soon be with.*

Well, I've got to go. I have to get some sleep because I'm going to start my training on the Switch Board tonight. Be sweet, work hard, stay "focused on our Future" and before you know it we'll be together again.

Love,
Robt.

Camp Evans Military Base (Communications Shop)

24 Jul 1970
Dear Bob Jr,

Bob, today I received your letter describing your response and my mom's response to the news about my new assignment to the Communications Shop. From what I read emotions were all over the place. Maybe I should have sent the letter with a box of tissues. Getting good news like that a few days after hearing about my mishap in the field could not have been timed any better. I knew my mom would get emotional. And I'm glad she was able to hear the good news from you. You know from reading my mom's letters I can see you two are really getting close. Going through this whole situation together will help the both of you develop a special relationship even before we are married. And I think that's the way it should be. Courtships should not just mold the relationship of the two individuals courting. It should also have a similar effect on the two families. Bob, most of all I was glad that the news brought you tears of happiness rather than tears of loneliness and worry.

Well, Babe, last night was my big night. I operated the Battalion Switch Board on my own. What I learned that was most important was not to miss the wakeup calls. They are very important. I'll say it again, "They are very important!" It could be for the Battalion Commander (Lt. Colonel) on down to a Staff Sergeant running the Helicopter Pad. After the first night operating the switch board I learned some do's and don'ts if you're pulling the night shift. (1) Do not take a hot shower after 6 P.M. (2) Do not eat anything heavy after evening chow. (3) Complete any naps or scheduled sleeping periods two hours prior to going on shift. You need to be awake and alert. (4) Do not try to write letters during your shift. Your attention will be on composing your letter and not on your wakeup calls, nor will you be ready to record messages.

Bob, the negative side of the job is the night shifts are long and lonely. But as long as I have your pictures to gaze at I have all the Company I need.

Love,
Robt.

Camp Evans Military Base (Communications Shop)

26 Jul 1970

Dear Bob Jr.

Today is Sunday and yes, I did go to Church this morning. In spite of being on bunker guard last night. I have a lot to be thankful for. Jesus once said, "Come as you are." So I went dirty, smelling of mosquito repellent, and with two large knots on my forehead from mosquito bites. But through all that I still enjoyed the service. And would you believe it, the message was "Stop and count your blessings."

Last night on Bunker Guard they put me on a position that called for an M-79 Grenade Launcher. So, I had two weapons my M-16 and a M-79. I didn't mind it because for a short time I carried an M-79 while in the field.

Well, Bob, what's going-on on Drake Street. Are the same people still hanging out together? Those that have asked about me please tell them I said "hello" and thank them for being concerned for my well-being. Mom wrote and told me about her and Mr. Donald getting married in September. I am very happy for them but I am very sad that I won't be able to attend. But I know you'll represent us both well.

Bob, I've got a problem right now, I can't get to sleep. After Church, I went straight to the showers but I was too late. The hot water was gone. So, I had to take a cold shower and now I'm sitting here wide awake. My goal is to try and get at least five hours of sound sleep before evening chow. I've got switchboard duty tonight so I need my z's.

Bob, when I look at your pictures the one thing I regret is that eventually I have to stop and put them away. I'm looking forward towards the day when I won't just be looking at a mere image of you but I'll have access to the real thing. I remember the words of Marvin Gaye, "Ain't nothing like the real thing baby." I'm looking forward to the day when I'm physically holding you in my arms again (the real thing). And I guarantee, at the end of the day I won't put you away!

Love,
Robt.

27 Jul – 26 Aug 70
No Letters Found for This Period

Camp Evans Military Base (Communications Shop)
27 Aug 1970
Dear Bob Jr,

Well, how's everything going? The wedding is only nine days away. Have you talked to my mother lately? How are Michael and Joyce taking this all in? I feel so left out. Make sure you write me that day and tell me all about it.

By now you should be getting ready to return to school. This will be your Junior Year so it should be all routine by now. This is probably your last week at work so along with the lifestyle transition there's also a mental transition that you'll have to go through. I'll write my last letter to your house on Sept. 1st until you send me your new school address.

Bob I've been quite busy these last few days getting my Jeep ready for an up-coming inspection. I have to paint it inside and out. The mechanic at the Motor Pool is working on my carburetor today. Yesterday I changed the oil filter and installed a new distributor. Since I've been driving a Jeep I have learned a lot about vehicle maintenance. I'll admit I will probably never know as much as some of the guys on Drake Street. But I know a lot more than I did in the past.

Bob, before I close I thought I'd let you know that I've got space in my photo album for about thirty of your pictures. So as of today, you have about 110 days to meet this request.

Well, I've got to go. It's chow time and I'm hungry. I'm scheduled for Bunker Guard tonight. After being subjected to those deadly mosquitoes there's no telling what I'll look like in the morning.

Love,
Robt.

28 Aug – 16 Oct 70
No Letters Found for This Period

Camp Evans Military Base (Communications Shop)
17 Oct 1970
Dear Bob Jr.

Good morning, Babe. It's Saturday morning and a very hot day. It's ten o'clock and already the temperature is 88-degress and the humidity is 86. ,, that's enough complaining about the weather one of the purposes of this letter is to congratulate you on "crossing over" into the Alpha Kappa Alpha Sorority (AKA). I know you've been going through the process of "pledging" for some weeks now and finally you have accomplished your goal. Other than you're being a part of a lifelong sisterhood I don't know very much about it. But if being an AKA was important to you then I 'm happy for you and

very proud of you. Plus, now you'll have more time to focus on your studies. Your graduating on time is very important to our future plans. I have to run for now. I think they're looking for me to get ready for my Switch Board shift. I really miss you!! Love & kisses.

Love,
Robt.

Camp Evans Military Base (Shop)
Communications
18 Oct 1970
Dear Bob Jr,
Bob, after our regular Church Service we had a
Memorial Service to honor those in our Battalion who died
in battle over the past three months. During the operations,
surrounding Firebase Ripcord and Firebase O'Reilly our
Battalion suffered significant casualties and several deaths,
including my best friend.
One thing that goes
through my mind is the
fact that they died so far
from home. Yes, they
had a military family but
that's not the same. We
have the privilege of
knowing when, how, and
why. And if they did not
die instantly we had the

privilege of being with them during their final moments.
That's where their families miss out.

 These soldiers were brave men who fought for their
country and more importantly for one another. Every
individual soldier understands that survival is not based on
the fittest but on the cohesiveness of the actions of the unit.
You can have superior weapons and tactical strategy, but
it's the individual resolve (purpose) and commitment
(engagement) of the individual soldier that wins the battles
and accomplishes missions.

 The average Infantry Soldier (grunt) has a High
School Education or less. But the bravery I've seen over
the past ten months cannot be taught in the halls of

Universities or the classrooms of Colleges. It can't be taught; it has to be developed. Bravery is the actions of an individual whose character has been developed with the capacity to be courageous when facing the challenges and hardships in life.

Today was a sad day because of the memory of their deaths. But it was also a good day because we set aside the time to honor their lives.

Bob we're down to two months to go. The Minister said today that, "If it were not for the mercy of God, those of us who are here today could have met the same fate." Regardless of all we've gone through, the combat situations, the loneliness of separation, and the fear/doubt, when we look back on it all, all I can say is "Thank God."

Love,
Robt.

19 Oct – 31 Oct 70
No Letters Found for This Period

Camp Evans Military Base (Communications Shop)
01 Nov 1970
Dear Bob Jr,

1:00 P.M. *Bob, this day started out to be very routine and with the exception of going to Church very dull. Last night I did an all-nighter on the Switch Board and looked at the guard roster only to discover that I have to go on Bunker Guard tonight.*

Bob, as I headed for the showers I heard all this yelling and cheering. Since I just had a towel wrapped around my waist I went into the Commo Shop to find out what all the commotion was about. Bob, I was so shocked at what they told me that I dropped my towel and exposed everything.

We were told last week that President Nixon was going to start drawing down on forces from the war. However, he's going to do it from both ends. Not only is he going to reduce the number of troops that will be sent to Vietnam. He's also going to shorten the tours of those currently in Vietnam. Bob, that means I could be leaving Vietnam earlier than December 17th (Michael's birthday). I'll know more at 4:00 P.M. So, I'll finish this letter then. I should have some more information. It doesn't look like I'm going to get any sleep today.

4:30 P.M. Well, Bob, it's true. And based on my official arrival date Dec. 21, 1969 I should be home just before Thanksgiving. I won't know for how long until I get my orders. Bob, can you believe it. It's almost over. Well, let me end this letter so I can get it in the mail today. Oh, of course you have the honors of telling my mom. I'll follow up with a letter to her tomorrow.

Love, Robt

P.S. Write your last letter to me on my birthday. I love you!!! Isn't it ironic? Since my birthday is on November 11th you'll be writing your last letter to me in Vietnam on Veterans Day.

Camp Evans Military Base (Communications Shop)

11 Nov 1970

Dear Bob Jr,

Bob, what a wonderful birthday present to be able to write my last letter from the Republic of South Vietnam. And I got your present in the mail yesterday. You had almost perfect timing. Thank you for my gifts. I'm listening to the Temptations right now and I've got the volume turned up as loud as it will go.

Okay, here's what I know right now regarding my departure from Vietnam. Depending on my flight I should be home as early as the 24th and no later than the 26th. (Thanksgiving Day). I don't want anyone to have to pick me up at the Airport. I'll catch a Cab home. Most Military flights are early in the morning. My flight will leave Vietnam from Camron Bay to Guam to Los Angeles and straight into Indianapolis. So, my total flight time will be about fifteen hours. If I get home on the 24th and you're still at school I would like to come to Muncie and get you for Thanksgiving. Bob, I can't wait to see you again. All I can say is you better have plenty of Chap Stick.

When the plane takes off from Camron Bay, I can imagine there will be a loud cheer. But after the flight levels off everybody will get quiet and just look out the window and reflect over the past year. We'll remember the friendships we made and the friends we lost. We'll reflect on the fire fights, the ambushes, the booby traps, all the combat and wonder how did "we" make it and others didn't. Like the other guys I won't be able to answer that. But I can thank God for his grace and mercy on me and pray for the families who lost their loved ones in a war so far away. But I think those of us that made it have learned

that life is precious and should not be taken for granted.
God has spared us for a purpose. So now we have a new
mission and purpose going forward, and we should take
full advantage of everyday to live out that purpose.

Bob, I'm going to take advantage of every second of
the leave time they give me to rekindle, or let's say
"strengthen", our love for each other. It's been a long year
for both of us to endure. We were fighting the uncertainty
of the War and the temptations and loneliness that come
with separation. I want to be sure that when I'm gone again
to serve out the last seven months of my Military Service
that our commitment to each other has not diminished but
is stronger than ever. After all, when this is all over we
have a destiny that can only be completed together. In
"1965" our love for each other was very strong and
sincere. I can't help but to believe that what we have just
endured has developed and strengthen our love for each
other to a level stronger and even more sincere than it was
then.

Bob, our relationship was a "model relationship"
when we were in high school and it will continue to be a
model relationship for our friends, children, and
grandchildren in the future. That is our new "Focus for the
Future". The next time you hear from me it will be ME!

Love,
Robt.

Section 4: Combat Development Experiment Command Fort Ord, California

Hunter Liggett Military Reservation
01 Jan 1971
Dear Bob Jr,

Happy New Year!! I 'm at my final destination, Hunter Liggett Military Reservation. And I am a little surprised at the living conditions. But after Vietnam, I will not complain about anything. The inner and outer walls of my barracks are plywood with a coat of paint. The windows are wire screen panels covered in plastic to keep the wind out. Inside the barracks at each end is a pot belly stove fueled by coal. This time of the year the temperature at night is in the upper 30's, and during the day it's in the low to mid 70's. I sleep on a twin bed in a sleeping bag. So, on cold nights there's the pot belly stove and during the heat of the day we have a small fan. The good news is the rest rooms and showers are in a brick enclosed building with glass windows and plenty of hot water. However, the building is about thirty meters from the barracks. This is home for the next seven and a half months. But it's clean and dry and a hundred times more comfortable than a foxhole in Vietnam. It's going to be a little lonely for a few days. I'm the first one here and no one else is due to arrive until Monday. I guess I'll spend the weekend getting

*familiar with the area.
The Sergeant Major did
inform me there will be
a total of twenty other
men in the barracks
with me and I will be
their Platoon Leader.*

*Bob, regardless of
all the time we spent
together and all the fun
we had, forty days was not enough. Now I am convinced
that we were born to be together. The only problem we had
was the lack of our own transportation. I don't care what
we did; going to church, going to the movies, going out to
dinner, going to different events, Attucks games or to our
favorite place; sitting in your den. Not only did we enjoy
being together but we looked good together. Your mother
even challenged us again when she asked, "Barbara Anne,
Robert, don't you two ever get tired of being together all
the time?" Again, our response to her was simply, "No,
ma'am." Our response to each other was, "That's why we*

*need to get
married." Bob,
what was really
surprising was
when we were out
and ran into
someone from high
school they were so
surprised that after
all this time we
were still together.*

And others still called us the model couple.

Bob, I was so proud to be with you. You always had on the right outfit for the occasion and yet you are a very modest dresser. You were so cute and petite, and you made the clothes look good. I'm glad I had two suits made in Vietnam or I would have been outclassed.

Bob, I even enjoyed the weekend when I came to Ball State for the line dance. I really enjoyed it. And you know how I generally feel about dances. Except for that one issue we discussed, it was a nice weekend. Your Sorority Sisters were very friendly and even some of the guys stopped and chatted with me. Most of them wanted to talk about the War. You must have showed everybody every picture I sent you. I know one thing everybody knew who I was. The only thing I (having fought in Vietnam as a member of the 101st Airborne Division) had an issue with was one of the Fraternities, as part of their outfit, wore Army Airborne jump boots spray painted in gold. I didn't say anything to you that night because I didn't want to seem critical, and I realized that was their thing and they had no idea that it might be offensive to anyone.

To sum it all up, I had a wonderful forty-day leave. I was able to spend most of the time with the girl that I love and we both realized that we will never be happy until we are permanently together. That was very evident on Thursday the day of my departure.

Bob, when we realized that we were about to be separated again both of our demeanors changed from happy and excited to sad and hurt. But Bob, I promise this will be the last time. And to help ease the pain and limit some of the letter writing I'll call you at least twice a week. You pick the days and times that best fit your schedule. However, because of the difference in time zones we'll have to coordinate the times. I'm going to try and call you tomorrow morning.

Bob, as soon as the plane took off I started missing you. When we leveled off at cruising altitude I reclined my seat closed my eyes and relived every moment we were together the past forty-days. Every kiss, hug, and smile.

Love,
Robt.

03 Jan – 21 Feb 71
No Letters Found for This Period

Hunter Liggett Military Reservation
22 Feb 1971
Dear Bob Jr,
I received your package today along with two nice letters. Thank you for the shirt. I love it. Now I have a hard

decision; do I wear it now or do I wait until I get home so you can see it on me. Decisions, decisions, decisions.

Bob, we had a five-day break from our current experiment. But we'll start up again tomorrow. I was really enjoying the time off, because riding in the back of a helicopter early in the morning this time of the year is miserable. It's so cold I wear a flight suit, gloves with liners, and my hands still get cold. The pilots don't have it too bad because they have some heating. This experiment will run until the 1st of May so maybe I'll get to enjoy some warm helicopter rides before it's over. Especially since no one's shooting at us.

Yes, Bob, I will call you at home during your quarter

break. And I'll make sure I have enough change so I won't have to call back collect. Just tell Sylvia if she answers the telephone to quit making me beg before she gives you the phone. Bob, I hate to hear that you're bored with school again. All I can say is hold on these next four and a half months and I promise you'll never be bored again. But I do understand what you mean about being bored. In my case it's the same routine every day. Get up in the morning, spend eight hours on the experiment, come back to the barracks, eat chow, and then you have a choice of playing basketball, going to the weight room, or going to the movies. You can go off base, but outside Hunter Liggett, other than getting a beer, there's not much to do. But again, I'm not complaining. After what I had to endure in Vietnam I can tolerate just about any routines or living condition. Bob, the only thing that I would have a real challenge dealing with is losing you. That would be so unthinkable that guess what, I'm not even going to think about it. Bob I'm thinking about our future together. When I get home, we'll sit down and plan every minute of our lives from that moment to the day we get married. I'll have a rough outline and we'll tweak it and fill it in together.

Love,
Robt.

23 Feb – 23 Mar 71
No Letters Found for This Period

Hunter Liggett Military Reservation
24 Mar 1971
Dear Bob Jr,
How are you today? I'm feeling pretty good, especially since I'll be calling you tomorrow. That means another week has gone by.

Yesterday, I was taking some guys through the parking lot on a "police call" and I saw a nice Mustang on sale for $1,400. Bob, it was really nice. It was a "66". The body was lime green with black leather interior and a black

vinyl top. The only thing that I wasn't too excited about was the bucket seats. You know that's not really our style. But we're getting a little older and mature so maybe our actions ought to reflect that (smile). Bob, I can picture you styling in one right now. What do you think? I'll talk to you about it tomorrow. I'm writing about it today because I'm kind of excited about it. Remember a car is the first purchase I'll make when I'm out of the service. I'll need it to get back and forth to work and to you on weekends!

Bob, I know how lonely it is for you waiting for me. But if you can endure it just a little while longer you'll never have to wait for me again. As a matter of fact, when I come home in July the tables will be turned. I'll be home waiting for you to finish your last year of college.

Bob, I miss you too, more than anything in the world. Just hold on and in the end, like the Bible say, "You'll get your just reward." And that will be a husband that will never stop loving you. ME!!! I love you.

Love,
Robt.

Hunter Liggett Military Reservation
11 Apr 1971
Dear Bob Jr,

Happy Easter!! Bob, how was your Easter Sunday? Mine was great. I've got a whole lot to be thankful for. I've survived a war and I have you. Do you remember our last Easter Sunday together in "69"? We couldn't get in Eastern Star Church so we went riding around. We came across a street vendor selling flowers, so we bought some for our mothers. We had a lot of fun that Easter. We were very happy and we had no idea what laid ahead for us in a few months. But it's almost over, Bob. Three months and days! Bob, you waited for me and when I come back we'll claim or reward, "each other". I love you, Bob.

I was looking, no, gazing, at the picture you sent me the other day. Bob, you have a small round face that's beautiful and lovely. When I look at your eyes they seem to be saying, "I love you, Robert." And when I look at your soft sweet lips they too seem to be saying, "I love you, Robert." Bob, love is all I'm asking from you for the rest of our lives. That's why I'm going to marry you. You're the only woman in the world that can give me the kind of love I'm looking for and need very much.

Bob, in your last letter you said that you would do more for me than ten of the finest women in the world. Bob, if I thought there were ten finer girls than you, I would be marrying one of them.

Also, in your last letter, you asked if I would be able to take care of a wife and children. Bob, you know I have always been able to manage money and make wise decisions. So, you don't have to worry about my ability to

159

take care of a wife and family. All you have to do is focus on taking care of the guy that's taking care of you and our family. And that's ME.

Bob, don't worry about your hair turning red. It won't have any effect on my love for you. Now, depending on how hot you look your changing hair color could have a major effect on my desire for you. I'll talk to you later on this week.

Love,
Robt.

Hunter Liggett Military Reservation
12 Apr 1971
Dear Bob Jr,

I know I just wrote you a letter last night, but I've got some great news. This morning during Company Formation the Company Commander called me out, "Specialist 4th Class Robert E. Wright, front and center." I marched up to him, saluted and said, "Specialist 4th Class Robert E. Wright reporting, Sir." He then said, "As of April 9, 1971, and because of the outstanding leadership you have demonstrated leading your Platoon, and the impeccable demonstration of sound character, you have been promoted to Sergeant (E-5)." I said, "Thank you, Sir." He then proceeded to remove my Specialist 4th Class Pins and replaced them with Sergeant Pins. Then he saluted me and said, "Sergeant Wright, great job, you are dismissed." Bob, I returned to my Platoon holding back the tears.

After the Company was dismissed, I was greeted by almost the whole company with their congratulations and well wishes. On my way, back to the barracks the Company

Commander wanted to see me in his office. Bob, when I arrived at his office he told me about a conversation that he had with our civilian contractor in charge of our experiment. They were very happy with the performance of the RTO's (Radio Telephone Operators) from the first Platoon. The CO told me he discussed the conversation with the Sergeant Major. The Sergeant Major said whatever actions demonstrated by the 1st Platoon is a direct reflection of their Platoon Leader, Specialist 4th Class Wright. He leads by example and has a reputation for his high level of integrity. The CO said that's one of the reasons I was up for promotion. He then stated that achieving the rank of E-5 with less than two years of service was very commendable. Bob, he then asked me if I had ever considered the Army as a career. I shared with him my future plans after completing my active Military Service obligation, which included marriage and my return to employment with Indiana Bell Telephone Company.

Bob, as you can see I have grown a lot in wisdom and character over the past two years. In your last letter you had questions regarding my ability to support and raise our family. I may be wrong but I don't think those doubts are coming from you. I think those seeds of doubt were sewn by others using the elitism of a college education over the training and development of military service. Bob you've heard one side of the argument now let me share with you my perspective. When I went to that line dance with you this is what I saw. I saw college boys dancing in spray-painted combat jump boots, but I've witnessed soldiers dying in the jungle in mud-covered combat boots. I saw college boys tapping candy-cane stripped sticks on the ground, but I've witnessed soldiers reloading their rifles magazine after magazine in fierce fire fights. I overheard college boys trying to decide how they were going to score with a defenseless half-drunk college girl, but I've witnessed a field medic make a snap decision on how he's going to keep a soldier from bleeding to death. I heard college boys talking about what they learned from this professor over that professor, but I've seen platoon leaders and squad leaders with high school educations read and navigate from complicated maps in order to have their unit in the right place to ensure the successful completion of a mission which saved many lives. Bob, I used all those illustrations not to put down or minimize the quality of education a college student receives. But on the other hand, I don't want anyone minimizing the level of training, development, and maturity of a combat soldier.

Bob, you know I am not the person I was in 1969. Over the past two years I have developed into a mature man who is not afraid to make decisions and take on responsibility. And Bob, when you add to that love, commitment, and devotion. You've got it all, Babe!!

Love,
Robt.

P.S. *Tell Sylvia that my promotion does not mean she has to call me "sir", but if I say "at ease" she has to stop messing with me (smile).*

Hunter Liggett Military Reservation
16 Apr 1971
Dear Bob Jr.

Bob, I had another great day today. First of all, I received two letters from you that put me in a very good mood. Regarding the first letter, we were tested and we prevailed, so let's just put that situation behind us and I'll just say, "All's forgiven in love and war."

Now let me share with you what happened to me this afternoon. After lunch, the Sergeant Major informed me that I had a meeting with the Battalion Commanding Officer (Lieutenant Colonel) at 1:30 P.M. When I arrived

at his office he greeted me with a handshake and a smile. Then he informed me of the purpose for the meeting. He had just received orders awarding me three distinct medals and commendations for my service in Vietnam, and he was honored to present them to me. He then presented me with the Army Commendation Medal, the Air Medal (2nd award) and the Bronze Star Medal. He pinned them on my chest and thanked me for my service. Now I have all my Medals. He also complemented me on my exemplary service record. For the next half hour, we talked about my tour in Vietnam.

Awards and Commendations:

- *Army Commendation Medal*
- *National Defense Service Medal*
- *Vietnam Service Medal*
- *The Bronze Star Medal*
- *The Air Medal (Second Award)*
- *Vietnam Campaign Medal*
- *Combat Infantryman's Badge*
- *Sharpshooters Badge M16 Rifle*
- *Certificate of Appreciation for Service in the Armed Forces of the United States from the United States Army Chief of Staff*
- *Certificate of Appreciation for Service in the Armed Forces of the United States from the President (Commander in Chief)*
- *Certificate of Service for serving in the Republic of Vietnam*

He ended the meeting asking me had I considered the

Army as a career. Bob, I shared with him our plans. He wished us luck in the future and I departed with a hand shake.

Bob, I hate to say it but I was very proud of myself today. When I went into the Army I was a nineteen-year-old immature kid. Two years later I'm a decorated Combat Veteran of the Vietnam War, a mature man. I have learned discipline, devotion to duty, honor, commitment, and leadership. All these attributes will be invaluable in civilian life. Whether it's living a disciplined life, devotion to my job, or committed to my wife (you) and family.

Bob, in addition to the Awards and Commendations I will receive an Honorable Discharge, which I'll need to go back to work. And I can take full advantage of the GI Bill. Which means money for College (night classes) and favorable credit and benefits when we buy our first home. As you can see I've always stayed "Focused on our Future".

Love,
Robt.

17 Apr – 14 Jul 71
No Letters Found for This Period

Fort Ord, California
15 Jul 1971
Dear Bob Jr,
Well, Bob, can you believe it, this will be my last letter. In five days, I'll be on my last flight home from Military Service and I will be hanging up my uniforms for good. This is one arrival that you can't miss. When you

jump into my arms we'll be entering into a new phase of our lives together.

    Bob, last night when I was lying in my bunk I did a little soul-searching and reflecting on the past two years, particularly my year in Vietnam. And I asked myself why me? How did I survive the violence, the hardships, and the separation from you? Bob, it was not easy. At times, I felt as if I was fighting three separate foes. And the more I thought about it, I was. Then I asked myself how I was victorious over three separate foes in the same War.

*As I thought about it, it all became clear. I used three different weapons. I used my "M-16" to fight the NVA and the Viet Cong, I used a "pen" to fight against the loneliness of separation, and I used my "faith" in God to fight fear and doubt. My M-16, pen and paper, and faith, those were my "**weapons of war.**" And Bob, you to played a major role in my survival. Your letters meant the world to me. They were inspirational and reassuring. They kept me focused and gave me strength and hope at a time when I needed it the most. Your letters were a constant reminder of the love we shared, and your pictures were a constant reminder of the person I was sharing it with.*

Bob, you should be getting out of school today. I'm so glad. When I get home, I want to spend as much time with you as I can before I go back to work and you go back to school. By the way, have you heard anything about the strike they're having at the telephone company? From what I'm hearing, my starting back to work may be delayed a week or two. That would also delay my getting a car. I've got the down payment, but I'll need to be working in order to get it financed. We'll see what happens. I might be able to work something out. If I can get proof of employment from the Telephone Company and push the first payment out as far as possible we might be okay.

Bob, I'm at Fort Ord, and I'll be processing out of the Army from here. I'll say one thing, it's a lot nicer than Hunter Liggett. It's very foggy today and from my window I can see the ocean. It's hard to believe that less than a year ago I was on the other side of that ocean. Bob the Army has helped me to realize just how much I love you and need you. In addition, the Army has also helped to develop me into the man that can appreciate, respect, and care for you. I really feel very blessed right now. I know God has been a part of all this. I think he is preparing me for something in the future (don't fret; I don't think you'll have to worry about being a preacher's wife). What, I don't know. I'm just so grateful that He's brought us back together again Now we can go back to being: Bob & Bob.

Love,
Robt.

Survived Vietnam

Completed Active Duty

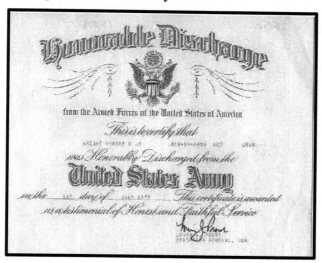

Married Bob Jr. - March 4, 1972

1982 - The Wright Family Bob Jr, Bob Sr, Nolise and Angela

Barbara's Letter to Robert

March 4, 1996

Dear Bob,

On this date 24 years ago I accepted you as my husband and I became your wife. Through the years I've watched you mature as a man. You've always been kind and gentle with me. You've avoided getting into major arguments. You've never hit me nor cursed at me. Thank you for staying with me this long.

I knew I was going to marry you when I was fifteen years old. I've never considered being with anyone else but you. I love you today as much as I loved you in 1965. I pray we'll always be together.

All my love, **Bob**

Barbara Anne Hampton Wright

Barbara departed this earthly life on December 31, 2002, at the age of fifty-two years, three months, and three days. She will be greatly missed by her family and friends. But no one will miss her more than the love of her life for thirty-seven years, her beloved Robert.

A Tribute to My Beloved Girlfriend, Fiancée, and Wife

To Bob Jr.,
Thank you for what you brought to my life:
Thank you for those wonderful times in high school because you were the first true love of my life.

Thank you for your faithfulness and love while I was serving in Vietnam for during a time of death and despair you brought hope and encouragement in my life.

Thank you for your love, patience, support and understanding during our thirty-one years of marriage because you brought a sense of purpose to my life.

Thank you for our two beautiful daughters; in them I will cherish living memories of you for the rest of my life.

Thank you for your commitment to Christ which brought direction and meaning to my life.

Prayer: Thank you, Lord, for your mercy and grace. Thank you for giving me what I did not deserve at a time when I needed it the most.

Love, Robert

Whoso findeth a wife findeth a good thing, and obtainth favor of the Lord Proverbs 18:22 KJ

The Author

Childhood: Born on "Veterans Day" November 11th 1949 in Indianapolis, Indiana. Grew up in Lockefield Gardens, an inner-city housing project located two miles west of downtown Indianapolis.

Education: June 1968 graduated from Crispus Attucks High School in Indianapolis, Indiana. May 1983 received a Diploma from Indiana Christian University in Old and New Testament Studies. May 10th 2014 received an Associates of Arts Degree majoring in "Leadership and Ministry" from Crossroads Bible College in Indianapolis, Indiana. May 9th 2015 received a Bachelor of Science Degree in "Church Management and Ethics" from Crossroads Bible College.

Work career: Started in 1968 as a Residential Installer with Indiana Bell Telephone Company. Retired as a Project Manager in Network Operations after 26 years of service October 1st 1994. October 2nd, started a new career as the Business Administrator at Eastern Star Church under the leadership of Senior Pastor Jeffrey A. Johnson Sr. September 1st 2000 promoted to Chief Operating Officer. Retired December 31st 2015 after 21 years of service in full-time Ministry. Currently serves on the Finance Team, the Church Council, and as Chairman of the Deacon Board.

Weapons of War was a project I enjoyed for several reasons. It brought back the memories of my youth, I can see how God has guided my steps and at the same time guarded my path, and if anyone has any questions about the Vietnam War I now have a story I can tell. A soldier's story.

In 2013, I was diagnosed with Parkinson's Disease. Dealing with that was not on my bucket list for retirement.

But God is good. I joined a program called Rock Steady Boxing. They have a fitness program that consists of non-contact boxing and core strength development to counter-act and even slow down the effects of the disease. I really enjoy it. Like Vietnam, Parkinson's is just another test that came at a different stage in life. But God is the same yesterday, today, and tomorrow. He's been with me through every stage of my life. As long as the curtain is up the show goes on.

Robert E. Wright
2018